Codependency Recovery Workbook

Go from Fear of Abandonment, People Pleasing, and Self-Neglect to Thriving in Healthy Relationships

© Copyright 2024 - All rights reserved.

The content contained within this book may not be reproduced, duplicated, or transmitted without direct written permission from the author or the publisher.

Under no circumstances will any blame or legal responsibility be held against the publisher or author for any damages, reparation, or monetary loss due to the information contained within this book, either directly or indirectly.

Legal Notice:

This book is copyright-protected. It is only for personal use. You cannot amend, distribute, sell, use, quote, or paraphrase any part of the content within this book without the consent of the author or publisher.

Disclaimer Notice:

Please note the information contained within this document is for educational and entertainment purposes only. All effort has been executed to present accurate, up-to-date, reliable, and complete information. No warranties of any kind are declared or implied. Readers acknowledge that the author is not engaging in the rendering of legal, financial, medical, or professional advice. The content within this book has been derived from various sources. Please consult a licensed professional before attempting any techniques outlined in this book.

By reading this document, the reader agrees that under no circumstances is the author responsible for any losses, direct or indirect, that are incurred as a result of the use of the information contained within this document, including, but not limited to, errors, omissions, or inaccuracies.

Free Bonus from Andy Gardner

Hi!

My name is Andy Gardner, and first off, I want to THANK YOU for reading my book.

Now you have a chance to join my exclusive email list related to human psychology and self-development so you can get the ebook below for free as well as the potential to get more ebooks for free! Simply click the link below to join.

P.S. Remember that it's 100% free to join the list.

Access your free bonuses here:
https://livetolearn.lpages.co/andy-gardner-codependency-recovery-workbook-paperback/

Or, Scan the QR code!

Table of Contents

INTRODUCTION 1
SECTION 1: UNDERSTANDING CODEPENDENCY 3
SECTION 2: UNPACKING THE FEAR OF ABANDONMENT 16
SECTION 3: THE COST OF SEEKING APPROVAL 31
SECTION 4: RECOGNIZING AND RECTIFYING SELF-NEGLECT 43
SECTION 5: BOUNDARIES AND CODEPENDENCY 55
SECTION 6: FINDING YOURSELF: THE JOURNEY TO SELF-DISCOVERY 68
SECTION 7: FROM CODEPENDENCY TO INTERDEPENDENCE 79
SECTION 8: COMMUNICATING TO IMPROVE INTERACTIONS WITH OTHERS 90
SECTION 9: SURVIVING AND THRIVING: HEALING THE PAST AND MAINTAINING HEALTHY RELATIONSHIPS 103
CONCLUSION 115
HERE'S ANOTHER BOOK BY ANDY GARDNER THAT YOU MIGHT LIKE 118
FREE BONUS FROM ANDY GARDNER 119
REFERENCES 120

Introduction

If you're reading this book, you're ready to let go of unhealthy relational patterns and learn how to build and maintain healthy relationships. Being in a codependent relationship keeps you stuck in an endless loop of neglecting your own needs in favor of the approval of others, a lack of self-understanding, and losing yourself in unhealthy relationship dynamics. Regardless of why you decided to pick up this book, it is certain that you're not alone in this journey. This workbook is crafted especially for you and everyone else who wishes to overcome patterns of codependency.

Codependency is very draining. It feels like issues like fear of abandonment, self-neglect, and people-pleasing tendencies are inescapable. This book aims to help you break free from these worries and live a life of renewed purpose, self-love, compassion, and healthy connections. This book isn't just about expanding your knowledge and helping you understand the reasons behind these struggles but is also designed to guide you through a transformative journey of personal growth, development, and self-discovery.

Reading the first section, you'll understand what codependency is, its causes, and how it manifests itself in relationships. You'll find a self-assessment quiz and several self-reflection exercises that will help you gain insight into your experiences. The following sections will guide you through the specific aspects of codependency, fear of abandonment, the overwhelming need for approval, self-neglect, and the lack of boundaries, and how to navigate each of these issues to work toward growth and healing.

As you progress through the book, you'll feel encouraged to explore your own identity, needs, wants, goals, and aspirations. You'll find a plethora of introspective exercises that will help you explore aspects of yourself that were hidden by your codependent tendencies and emotionally demanding relationships. In the last section, you will understand the relationship between your upbringing, traumas, and codependency and find several techniques and activities that will help you let go of what no longer serves you. You'll understand what healthy relationships look like and feel empowered to take actionable steps to build a healthy, purposeful, and independent life for yourself.

After reading this book, you will understand that other people's opinions and approval don't decide your value and worth. You will understand how to gain the respect of others and establish healthy boundaries that make you feel mentally, emotionally, and physically secure. Dive into the following chapters with an open mind and heart and trust in your own transformative power.

Section 1: Understanding Codependency

In this section, you'll learn what codependency is and how it can impact your mental and emotional health. You'll discover the psychological reasons behind the development of this tendency and how it manifests itself in relationships. You'll understand the signs of being in a codependent relationship and know how this tendency enables or encourages other people's negative behaviors toward you.

Codependency is an unhealthy form of interaction in a relationship.
https://unsplash.com/photos/woman-on-bike-reaching-for-mans-hand-behind-her-also-on-bike-AsahNlC0VhQ

It also explores the differences between healthy and codependent relationships. Finally, you'll find several activities within the chapter that help you determine whether you have codependent tendencies, reflect on how they might have been influenced by your family, and assess their impact on your overall well-being.

What Is Codependency?

Codependency is an unhealthy form of interaction that can take place in any type of relationship, whether romantic, familial, or social. In this dynamic, one individual becomes the giver in the relationship, and the other becomes the taker. The former abandons their own wants and needs to the point where they completely neglect their personal well-being for the sake of the taker's wants, needs, and well-being.

In many cases, codependency is a behavior that the affected individual learns during their upbringing. It's a profound issue that can significantly impact quality of life and is therefore classified as an emotional and behavioral condition. Codependent individuals are unable to maintain healthy relationships with others because they're inclined to give more than they receive. This behavior leads to a one-sided relationship, which can become emotionally destructive for the person who assumes the role of the giver. Codependent relationships also often lead to exploitation or abuse.

One or both individuals in a codependent relationship may experience poor mental health. A lack of self-esteem, feelings of underachievement, immaturity, and irresponsibility are common traits that arise on both sides, perpetuating codependent behaviors. In some codependent relationships, both parties may assume the role of the giver. They may both dedicate their entire lives to the relationship and direct all their time and effort toward pleasing the other person. By doing so, the giver jeopardizes other areas of their life and causes potential damage to other relationships, academic or professional success, health and well-being, and may neglect daily chores or responsibilities.

Regardless of who assumes which role, both individuals are considered codependent in this relationship dynamic. One person depends on the sense of self-worth and achievement they receive from taking care of the person, while the person being taken care of depends on the validation, assistance, support, and other forms of help they receive from the giver. Both people heavily rely on the benefits they receive from the other, making it difficult for each to thrive independently.

Codependency is a lot more than being highly dependent on another person. It's also characterized by enmeshment. This means that the identities of both people in the relationship are deeply intertwined with each other. Maintaining this dynamic for long periods of time can make both parties unaware of who they are without each other. In case of a breakup, one or both people struggle to remember who they were before the relationship existed. The healing process is often a long period of self-discovery, where one or both people relearn who they are without the other person. They rediscover their wants, needs, hobbies, talents, preferences, goals, interests, and much more.

Someone in a codependent relationship isn't necessarily unable to take care of themselves. Many of those in codependent marriages are able to work, earn a living, pay the bills, and provide for their homes and children. However, they have an unhealthy attachment to another person and depend on them to feel secure, worthy, successful, or lovable.

The Psychological Roots of Codependency

A codependent individual's sense of self-worth is entirely tied to their ability to help, support, or even fix others, creating a severe gap or imbalance in the relationship. When the other person finds that they're being taken care of regardless of the amount of effort they exert in a relationship, they eventually stop doing their part and contributing and assume their role as the taker. No one should ever depend on someone else to validate their worth. Many codependent individuals stay in unfulfilling and unhealthy relationships simply because the other person refuels their sense of purpose and boosts their self-esteem.

Childhood Trauma

People often develop codependency because of childhood trauma. Trauma has a plethora of long-lasting effects on the affected individuals and impacts how they interact with the world around them. People usually develop codependency as a result of feeling fundamentally flawed. They feel they must please everyone around them and constantly shower them with acts of service in order to feel loved, worthy, accepted, and valued. Codependent individuals may have been taught they must look out for others and care for them before replenishing their own wants and needs. They may have been made to feel that caring for yourself is selfish, which is why they become unhealthily dependent on others for external validation. Since they feel intrinsically flawed and underachieved, they constantly need others to tell them that their thoughts, feelings, interests, beliefs, and actions are right and valid.

We carry our childhood trauma into adulthood, and this contributes to codependency.
https://unsplash.com/photos/boy-covering-his-face-while-standing-svSclvGGJv4

Others who have experienced trauma may use codependency as a way to subconsciously protect themselves from traumatic experiences. They feel that codependency gives them control over their environment, which keeps them safe from trauma or abuse. Traumatic or negative experiences that lead to anxiety, insecurity, or low self-esteem, and therefore lead to codependency, include the death of a parent, extreme bullying, growing up with narcissistic or abusive parents, abandonment, a history of addiction in the family, and enmeshed family dynamics.

Unhealthy Attachment Styles

Codependency issues can also arise from a person's attachment style. The attachment theory suggests that the relationships people have with their caregivers during childhood greatly affect the ones they form during adolescence and adulthood. Individuals whose mental, emotional, and physical needs were met during childhood are generally able to build secure and healthy relationships as adults. Those whose psychological needs were unmet are more likely to have insecure attachment styles. This type of relationship dynamic results in unhealthy feelings and behaviors that influence the quality of their relationships. These feelings and behaviors may include a fear of rejection or abandonment, the desire to earn external validation, or emotional avoidance. These attributes can result in situations where the individual feels the need to cater to another person's wants and needs to enhance their own feelings of self-worth, gain approval, or improve their sense of identity. This results from entrenched beliefs that their self-worth is directly affected by their ability to meet the needs of others.

The Need to Be a Savior

Being in a relationship with someone who struggles with addiction, mental health conditions, or other issues that require them to be dependent on substances or certain individuals can make a person's codependency issues worse. This prods away at the giver's savior complex, creating a sense of urgency to help the struggling individual and cater to their needs. They'll feel solely responsible for saving the suffering individual, which, of course, is extremely emotionally demanding.

Modeled Behavior

Many people engage in codependency because it was modeled to them. It's what they've witnessed their parents or caretakers doing and has become all they've ever known. They grew up thinking that is how everyone should behave in a relationship and had no one to portray or explain to them what a healthy relationship should actually be.

Activity: Family Reflection

Reflecting on your family dynamics is crucial for self-awareness and development. Since codependency is often a result of childhood trauma or experiences, you need to explore any existing patterns that may give you insights into your relationships and codependency patterns.

1. Create a list of your extended family:

Parents:_____

Siblings:_____

Grandparents:_____

Aunts:_____

Uncles:_____

Cousins:_____

List other key figures, such as guardians or godparents, who might have deeply influenced your personality or behaviors:

_____

_____

_____

_____

2. Determine key relationships:

Now that you have a visual representation of your family, determine which people impacted your upbringing most.

_____

_____

_____

_____

3. Notice the dynamics:

Answer the following questions for each of the key relationships you determined:

- Did they enable (cover for, tolerate, or turn a blind eye to) any of your negative behavior? Did you notice that they enabled others?

    Example: Your sister pretended not to see you whenever you did something wrong, or your aunt always covered for her alcoholic husband.

_____

_____

_____

_____

- Did they take on excessive caretaking responsibilities?

  Example: Your mom always catered to your dad's wants and needs, ensuring he always felt satisfied, even when it compromised her own mental, physical, or emotional health.

  _____

  _____

  _____

  _____

- Did they openly discuss their emotions, or were they more likely to suppress them?

  _____

  _____

  _____

  _____

- Did you set boundaries with them? Did they respect your boundaries and those of others?

  _____

  _____

  _____

  _____

4. Identify your codependency triggers:

Reflect on situations that influenced your family dynamics and caused you, or others within the family, to exhibit codependent tendencies. How did these dynamics influence how you interact with others and approach relationships?

_____

_____

_____

_____

Signs You're in a Codependent Relationship

- Nothing outside your relationship makes you feel purposeful or satisfied. You readily turn down invites to hang out with your friends and family because you'd rather be with your partner.
- You go beyond admiring your partner's good qualities. You put them on a pedestal and often turn a blind eye to their flaws.
- You try to control your partner's behavior and get them to do what you want.
- You take the blame and apologize for everything, even if it's not your fault, because you would rather do that than get into an argument.
- You feel guilty whenever you're unable to fix one of your partner's problems or cater to all their wants and needs.
- You tolerate their negative behaviors, such as verbal or physical abuse, and defend their actions.
- You feel responsible for taking care of your partner and ensuring their comfort. You may do all the chores and pay the bills yourself, even if they're capable of pitching in.
- You cover for their poor choices and behaviors and are always there to defend and bail them out.
- You obsessively think about your partner's thoughts and feelings. Your mood also mirrors theirs. You're only happy when they are, and you're automatically down if they feel sad.
- You fear triggering a conflict, so you avoid discussing your thoughts, feelings, needs, and wants with them. You would rather feel neglected and suppress your emotions than potentially upset your partner.
- You worry about expressing beliefs and interests that don't align with your partner's in fear that they might bully you or view you in a negative light.

Activity: Codependency Checklist

Check all the statements that apply to you. Admitting these facts can be difficult. However, you must be honest with yourself to start on your healing journey.

- You struggle to say "no" to others. You find it hard to turn down requests even if they don't align with your needs, wants, and interests.
- You struggle with low self-esteem.
- You actively seek validation and approval from others.
- You often exhibit people-pleasing behaviors. You need other people to like you.
- You have an overwhelming fear of abandonment.
- You have a strong fear of rejection.
- You struggle to set and maintain boundaries with others.
- Your sense of self-worth depends on what others think of you.
- You struggle to express your thoughts, feelings, needs, and wants, especially if you think doing so might upset others.
- You feel responsible for other people's emotions.

Codependency Enables Negative Behaviors

In healthy relationships, people are expected to support and help each other whenever they need it. They should also guide and aid one another to grow and learn from their experiences. In codependent relationships, on the other hand, only the giver offers to help. They also take it upon themselves to fix the other person and make them feel comforted and supported regardless of their behavior. While this comes from a place of love and care, it can be extremely harmful to the other person because it also enables their unhealthy behavior. They will expect you to tolerate them and continue to help and support them, which discourages them from trying to help themselves.

Codependent individuals struggle with an overwhelming need to be needed. Assuming the role of the savior and benefactor encourages the other person in the relationship to become or stay dysfunctional. Codependents fear that the other person will get better – whether in terms of employment or recovery from a mental or physical ailment – because it would mean they would no longer depend on the giver. If the other person becomes independent, the giver feels like they've lost their purpose and are no longer worthy of appreciation and love. An example of enabling would be a wife covering for her alcoholic husband and making sure he always feels supported. A dad who makes up excuses for their child's bad behavior is another example of enabling.

Continuously rescuing someone from the consequences of their actions and tolerating their negative behaviors encourages them to stay on a destructive course. They'll always depend on you to save and take care of them. If you struggle with codependency, this will increase your sense of reward, achievement, and satisfaction because you'll feel needed. Over time, you'll view yourself as the victim or a martyr and continuously seek out relationships with the same dynamic.

Healthy vs. Codependent Relationships

Many people confuse codependency for love, especially if this was the type of behavior modeled for them throughout their childhood. When people have been good friends or partners for a long time, it's normal for them to depend on each other in various areas of their lives. This, however, instantly becomes unhealthy if any of their lives revolve around that relationship and if it's prioritized over everything else. When you place extreme importance on one relationship, you sacrifice everything for it and set unrealistic expectations for the other person. You also attempt to control the relationship dynamic by being codependent, and when that doesn't work - or you don't yield the response you want - you may become disappointed or even resentful.

Being codependent can't be described as being clingy either, as clinginess is something everyone experiences at some point or another. It's normal to want to be near your partner and to want their attention sometimes. However, planning your entire life around your relationship and your partner's availability is harmful. Codependent individuals do whatever it takes, even if it means sacrificing their own well-being for their partners" happiness and satisfaction.

Many confuse codependency for love.
https://unsplash.com/photos/woman-holding-man-hand-Y3L_ZQaw9Wo

Healthy relationships, however, are characterized by independence. It encourages both parties to find and maintain a balance between their identity, thoughts, and feelings, those of the other party, and those that arise in the relationship. Both individuals contribute to the relationship and equally depend on each other while respecting each other's independence and uniqueness.

In a healthy relationship, each person has different emotions that are equally valued, validated, and respected. In a codependent relationship, the emotions of both partners are enmeshed and deeply entangled. That can lead to confusion, frustration, and feeling misunderstood. Healthy relationships are characterized by balancing your activities and interests and having your partner support your emotional needs. Codependent individuals, however, expect their emotional needs to be completely fulfilled by the other person. Without them, the codependent individual has low self-esteem, no inner validation, a lack of a sense of purpose, and low self-worth. A healthy individual's self-worth and purpose don't depend on external validation.

Healthy love encourages each individual to have and maintain their own identity, as both people celebrate and appreciate each other's differences. Both understand they won't always have overlapping interests, desires, hobbies, and friends. Codependents, on the other hand, believe that they must always have an identity that aligns with that of their partners. In healthy relationships, each partner feels empowered to make their own decisions, while codependents use fear, shame, and guilt-tripping to influence each other's decisions. Finally, healthy individuals respect each other's boundaries, while codependent individuals feel threatened whenever their partner instills a boundary.

When a person is so focused on fulfilling someone else's needs and leaves no room for either individual's independence, it can be very hard to work toward personal success. Codependent individuals don't understand how intense of a buffer they're putting on their own lives by being so focused on someone else. However, it's difficult to comprehend the gravity of the situation and its consequences when you're in it.

Naming certain situations and social or mental issues, such as codependency, can help you define negative behaviors. It also validates your thoughts and feelings and reassures you that they're not alone. On the other hand, since not everyone understands a codependent person's thoughts, feelings, and overall situation, the term "codependency" has become, to an extent, loaded with judgment. This is why many people who realize they're struggling with codependency can feel like it's something they should be embarrassed about. These feelings of shame and embarrassment can discourage them from seeking help. Codependency can happen to everyone and is nothing to be ashamed of.

Healthy Relationships

Humans were made to be social beings who thrive in groups and communities. Hardly anyone can survive on their own. There is nothing wrong with supporting and helping others as long as you can ask for and receive help. In healthy, interdependent relationships, both people must give and take support, aid, and encouragement.

On some days, you'll give 50% and take 50%. On other days, you'll give 80% and receive 20%. That's fine as long as you know that on days you're only able to contribute 30%, 20%, or 10% to the relationship, your partner will give the rest. While relationships must be balanced, it doesn't mean you'll both be able to give each other an equal amount of time and effort daily. It means that both of you must be willing to step up when either of you is struggling to make things work. In a codependent relationship, only one person is expected to always give the most effort. That person fears that if they can no longer sustain these efforts, their partner will not do anything to save the relationship. Giving without receiving will eventually lead to burnout and resentment, no matter how much you love your partner.

Being in an independent relationship increases your self-esteem and self-worth. You realize you don't need to earn anyone's love, appreciation, or respect. Healthy relationships offer emotional and mental safety because you don't have to constantly wonder whether you're doing enough to satisfy your partner. Most importantly, independence encourages you to have your own identity, which is crucial for happiness and success. Those in codependent relationships barely pursue their passions, especially if they don't align with their partners'.

Activity: Codependency and Well-Being Check

Rate each of the following statements on a scale of 1 (strongly disagree) to 5 (strongly agree):

1. I prioritize other people's needs and wants over my own. __
2. My sense of self-worth depends on the approval I receive from others. __
3. My self-esteem depends on other people's opinions of me. __
4. I feel guilty when I set boundaries with others. __
5. I feel responsible for uplifting others and generally enhancing their emotions. __
6. I feel anxious when someone I care about is upset and wonder if it's because of me. __
7. I always ask for other people's opinions when making my own decisions. __
8. I constantly worry that others might reject or abandon me. __
9. I feel guilty when I say "no" to others. I often do what they want, even when it jeopardizes my well-being. __
10. My relationships significantly affect my overall well-being. __

If most of your answers are either 4 (agree) or 5 (disagree), that could indicate high codependent tendencies and potentially strongly impact your overall well-being.

Now that you've read this chapter, you understand what codependency is, the reasons behind it, and how it manifests. You have a strong idea of whether you're codependent, how strong these tendencies are, and their impact on your overall well-being.

Section 2: Unpacking the Fear of Abandonment

No one wants to be rejected or feel they aren't loved or needed. You want to trust your loved ones and know they will never turn their back on you or walk away. You may have people in your life who love and care about you, but you constantly worry they will leave you. You can't turn these thoughts off despite how much they reassure you.

It is normal to worry that your partner may break up with you after an ugly fight or that you will lose touch with a friend when they move to another country. However, when these fears take over your life, they can ruin your relationships.

The fear of someone leaving us creates many long-lasting mental issues.
https://unsplash.com/photos/man-holding-luggage-photo-g1WdcKcV3w

Fear of abandonment can cause severe anxiety and ruin your self-esteem. You don't have to live this way. This chapter explores the origin and manifestations of this fear and what you can do to overcome it.

What Is Fear of Abandonment?

Fear of abandonment is a persistent voice inside your head telling you, "Everyone you love will leave you." It is a type of anxiety characterized by an overwhelming fear that makes you believe all your relationships are doomed to end. This complex emotion stems from early childhood experiences or past relationship traumas. For instance, if your father left you as a child, you may have developed a fear of abandonment, believing that your family, friends, romantic partner, etc., will eventually leave you too.

Although it is an irrational fear, fear of abandonment isn't a phobia. It is very common and can have a damaging impact on every area of your life. People with this fear usually develop unhealthy patterns of thoughts and behavior that affect how they interact with their loved ones. Without realizing it, they push everyone they love away and sabotage their relationships, resulting in their worst fear coming true. Others are so afraid of getting hurt that they build a wall around them to prevent anyone from getting close. This makes it hard for them to be in healthy relationships.

Types of Fear of Abandonment

Whether physical or emotional, there is more than one type of fear of abandonment.

Physical Abandonment

This is one of the most common types. It's when you are afraid that someone you love will walk away from you. This can be your partner leaving or divorcing you or a friend cutting ties with you.

Emotional Abandonment

This one is less obvious, but it can be equally or more traumatic than physical abandonment. It is usually the result of a parent who was physically present but emotionally absent. They ignore their child's emotional needs, making them feel neglected, unappreciated, disconnected, unloved, and alone.

For instance, if your parents were unaffectionate or dismissed your feelings when you were hurt, you may have developed a fear of abandonment.

Fear of Abandonment in Children

All babies and toddlers scream and cry when their parents leave the room because they don't know if they will return or not. This is a type of separation anxiety, and it is a normal phase that all children experience. However, some never outgrow this feeling and grow up fearing separation.

Fear of Abandonment in Relationships

This usually occurs when you become suspicious of your partner for no good reason. You believe that they may be cheating on you or are planning to leave you. As a result, you keep an emotional distance from them to protect yourself from getting hurt, or you drive your partner away with your accusations.

Reasons Behind Fear of Abandonment

Fear of abandonment usually stems from a traumatic event that happened in your childhood. An unsafe environment, inadequate emotional support, and a lack of affection make children grow up believing they can't trust anyone. The only thing they know is abandonment, so they live in constant fear of getting hurt again.

Childhood Trauma

Children who go through a traumatic experience like sexual, physical, or emotional abuse believe that they are unworthy of love. As adults, they subconsciously choose abusive partners because this is the only treatment and type of relationship they know.

Other types of childhood trauma include parental neglect, divorce, or a loved one death. These damage their ability to feel safe in a relationship. Children with a normal upbringing understand that neither distance nor conflict can damage a relationship. Childhood trauma can make them believe that their relationships are fragile and can easily be damaged, leading to a fear of abandonment.

Past Experiences

As you grow up, you experience changes and losses like a best friend moving to another city, a sibling moving out, or a bad breakup. These are normal events that can happen to anyone. Most people learn to adapt. Others, however, never move on and spend their lives grieving the losses. Even though they have never experienced abandonment, these normal events can trigger this fear.

Mental Health Conditions

Mental health conditions like avoidant personality disorder, dependent personality disorder, separation anxiety disorder, and borderline personality disorder can heighten fear of abandonment.

Symptoms of Fear of Abandonment

- Codependency
- Shallow relationships
- Commitment issues
- Sabotaging relationships
- Staying in toxic relationships due to fear of being alone
- Constant reassurance
- Quick attachment
- Insecure attachment style
- Repressed anger
- Self-blame
- Low self-esteem
- Feeling unworthy of love
- Fear of intimacy
- Trust issues
- Dreading the thought of being alone
- People pleasing
- Insecurity
- Jealousy
- Anxiety and depression
- Sensitivity to criticism
- Difficulty making friends

The Impact of Fear of Abandonment on Relationships

Even if you are in a committed relationship with someone who loves you and reassures you every day, you can still develop a fear of abandonment due to your childhood trauma. This fear distorts your sense of reality and makes you believe that your partner will leave you one day. You may develop trust issues, and slowly, these issues become an obsession that can ruin your relationship.

For instance, your partner is up for a promotion and is working hard, so you barely see them. You tell yourself they are either cheating on you or are planning to leave you. You confront them about it, but no matter what they say and do to convince you they are just busy with work, you don't believe them. You keep pressuring them, and they feel torn between trying to make you happy and focusing on their job.

Eventually, the constant fighting and accusations drive them away. You may even believe that your relationship is ending anyway, so you leave them before they abandon you.

Constant arguments can be one of the reasons people walk away.
https://unsplash.com/photos/silhouette-of-man-and-woman-under-yellow-sky-7KQc_8Mcex8

You keep repeating the same patterns in all your relationships, and you end up believing that everyone abandons you when, in reality, you are unintentionally sabotaging your relationships.

People with a fear of abandonment enter relationships with one foot out of the door. They spend the whole time believing that their partner will break up with them. They convince themselves they are unlovable or unlucky in love. Without understanding their thought patterns, they keep going from one relationship to the next, continuing the toxic cycle.

You may experience the same challenges with your other relationships. You may feel distressed if a friend becomes close to someone else, and you start acting jealous or clingy.

People Pleasing

Fear of abandonment can push you to become a people pleaser. You will go out of your way to make others happy by becoming overly agreeable or too accommodating. You sacrifice your own happiness and comfort to please them. You ignore your boundaries and struggle with saying "no" because you are afraid they will leave you if you do.

For instance, your best friend calls you and asks you to drive her to the airport tomorrow morning. You have a job interview, and you can't reschedule. If you refuse, you are afraid they will get mad, so you agree at the expense of missing the interview and losing a great opportunity. Had you told your friend the truth, they would have understood and just called an Uber.

Clinginess

You may exhibit clingy behavior, like constantly asking for reassurance. You may ask things like, "Will you ever leave me?" "I would do anything for you. You love me and would do anything for me, right?" "You haven't said you love me in a while. Do you still feel the same way?"

You may also call them multiple times a day, even when they are busy at work, and get mad when they don't answer. You may accuse them of not loving you enough if they go out with their friends without taking you. You feel jealous of anyone getting close to them because you worry they may take them away from you.

Quick Attachments

You always get attached too quickly, whether it's a new friend or a relationship. You start spending all your time together and sharing intimate details with them. Your relationships become intense, and you feel as if you have known them your whole life. However, these relationships fade as quickly as they begin.

Testing Your Loved Ones

Asking if a person still loves you may not always be enough to reassure you. You may take things a step further by testing the people in your life. For instance, you may stop taking your best friend's calls or refuse to reply to their messages to see if they worry about you or not. This acts as a validation that this person will always be there for you.

Some people may even cheat on their partners to see if they will still stay with them after they have been unfaithful or not.

Pattern of Unhealthy Relationships

You are usually attracted to abusive partners who will end up hurting you to recreate the cycle of abuse you experienced as a child. You may choose someone who is an addict, a workaholic, or someone emotionally unavailable (IE., *isn't over their ex*).

You believe that if someone truly knows you, they won't love or accept you. So, you keep people at a distance. You never show your vulnerable side or confide in them with your secrets. As a result, you may feel lonely in all your relationships.

Emotional Toll of Fear of Abandonment

Fear of abandonment not only ruins your relationships but can also take a toll on your mental health and self-esteem.

Anxiety

People suffering from a fear of abandonment often experience severe anxiety in their relationships. They constantly overthink everything their partner says or does and worry that they may be abandoned. They also need to be around their partner all the time, or they may experience separation anxiety. They also experience attachment anxiety, which results from fear of rejection and abandonment. This can lead to needy and clingy behavior.

Low Self-Esteem

Children who were abandoned by their parents often blame themselves. They may have been too young to make sense of what happened, so they feel that their parents didn't love them enough or they did something wrong to push their parents away. They grow up with no self-esteem. They may also believe they deserve to be abandoned, leading to self-loathing.

Confident people rarely experience fear of abandonment. If you believe in yourself, knowing you are good enough and deserve to be loved, you won't worry about being abandoned. However, fear of abandonment distorts your reality. You don't see how smart or funny you are. You see yourself in a negative light and only focus on your flaws, some of which aren't even real.

Unhealthy Coping Mechanisms

People with a fear of abandonment may develop poor or even harmful communication skills as coping mechanisms to deal with anxiety. For instance, you feel that your partner is acting differently. Instead of talking to them and finding out what's wrong, you resort to attention-seeking behavior, like trying to make them jealous.

Oversensitivity

Say your best friend tells you to ease down on your drinking because you embarrassed them at their engagement party. Instead of apologizing for your behavior, you get defensive and accuse them of always criticizing you when this is the first time they have mentioned it.

Fear of abandonment can make you overly sensitive to feedback and criticism. You believe that any comment on your actions or behaviors means people don't love you and will leave you. *Criticism triggers your fear of rejection,* so you act defensively to compensate for – or mask – your vulnerability.

Some people who suffer from fear of abandonment are perfectionists. They believe if they are perfect, everyone will love them. That isn't realistic, and they end up feeling anxious and tense all the time. They also struggle with criticism. For instance, your boss tells you your last project wasn't your best work. You take this comment personally, believing that there must be something wrong with you if your work is flawed.

Excessive Worrying Over Your Loved Ones

People who live with unresolved abandonment issues may worry obsessively about the people in their lives, especially when it comes to their safety. They always tell their partner to call them when they get to work to ensure they arrive safely. They may also live in fear that a loved one will get sick or in an accident and die.

This can suffocate the people in their lives with the constant checking-in and unnecessary worrying. This leads to tension, constant fighting, and instability in the relationship.

Excessive worry and overthinking can be suffocating for those around you.
https://unsplash.com/photos/woman-in-white-tank-top-NW61v3xF0-0

Healing requires you to acknowledge and validate your feelings. It may be hard to come face-to-face with the truth about your fear of abandonment and how it makes you behave in relationships. However, it is necessary to accept these feelings as a part of your journey. Don't be ashamed of them or dismiss them. What caused your fear of abandonment wasn't your fault. You are merely a victim of unfortunate circumstances. You didn't have any control back then. Your fear is like a bandage hiding your wounds and protecting you from pain. Once you heal, you won't need it.

So, embrace this part of yourself and practice self-compassion.

Activities

These activities will help you understand your fear of abandonment so you can start taking the necessary steps to overcome it.

Self-Reflection

Sit in a quiet room and consider your relationships with your family, friends, co-workers, partners, etc. Have you exhibited any specific behaviors that might be driven by a fear of abandonment?

_____

_____

_____

If you can't think of anything, try answering these questions.
1. When was the last time you said "No" to someone?

_____

_____

_____

2. Do you prioritize other people's happiness over your own?

_____

_____

_____

3. Do you get attached to people quickly?

_____

_____

_____

4. Do you always experience trust issues in your relationships?

_____

_____

_____

5. Do you often ask the people in your life for reassurance?

_____

_____

_____

_____

6. Have you ever tested your friends or partners to see how far they will go for you?

_____

_____

_____

_____

_____

7. Do you often find yourself in unhealthy relationships?

_____

_____

_____

_____

_____

8. Are you committed in your relationships, or do you subconsciously wait for them to end?

_____

_____

_____

_____

_____

9. Do you get insecure when your partner or friends spend their time with someone else?

_____

_____

_____

_____

10. If you didn't have a fear of abandonment, what would your relationships look like?

_____

_____

_____

_____

Read your answers back and reflect on them.

Meditation to Calm Your Fear

Instructions:
1. Find a quiet room with no distractions.
2. Wear something soft and loose-fitting.
3. Set your timer for 15 or 20 minutes.
4. Sit in a cross-legged and relaxed position with your back straight. You can sit against a wall or on a chair.
5. Take a few deep breaths and feel the air fill your lungs before you exhale.
6. Repeat a mantra that aligns with your intention, like "I am free of fear."
7. Focus on every word as you breathe.
8. Change your breathing pattern to practice breath of fire.
9. Breathe in through your nostrils and fill your belly with air.
10. Don't pause and forcibly breathe out through your nose.
11. Repeat for a couple of minutes.

12. Focus on how the breathing and chanting are making you relaxed.
13. If your mind wanders, bring back to your mantra and breathing.
14. After you have finished, take a long and deep breath, raise your arms, and exhale.

Visualization
Instructions:
1. Find a quiet room.
2. Sit or lie down and close your eyes.
3. Visualize yourself lying on a beach.
4. You are all alone and can only hear the sound of the waves.
5. You feel the warm sand under your feet and the cool breeze on your face and hair.
6. Feel your body sinking in your chair.
7. Feel your body relax and let go of all the tension.
8. Keep breathing with the rhythm of the waves.

Overcoming Your Fear of Abandonment

Overcoming the fear of abandonment will take time and effort. Believe in yourself and that you have it in you to put the past behind you and heal.

Practice Self-Compassion

Many people feel ashamed of their fear of abandonment. They judge themselves harshly when they become aware of their behavior and feelings. Develop self-love and self-compassion so you can become better equipped to handle your fear. You can do this by reframing your thoughts. Instead of saying, "I am not lovable," say, "I am loved." Instead of saying, "People always abandon me," say, "I am worthy of love."

Set Healthy Boundaries

Set healthy boundaries and start taking care of yourself and your needs. Learn to say "No" when something inconveniences you or makes you uncomfortable. Understand that your relationship won't end when you deny someone their request. Let people know how you want to be treated and that you won't tolerate any disrespect. Suppose someone constantly tries to cross your boundaries and use your fear of abandonment against you. In that case, they are probably toxic, and you don't need them in your life.

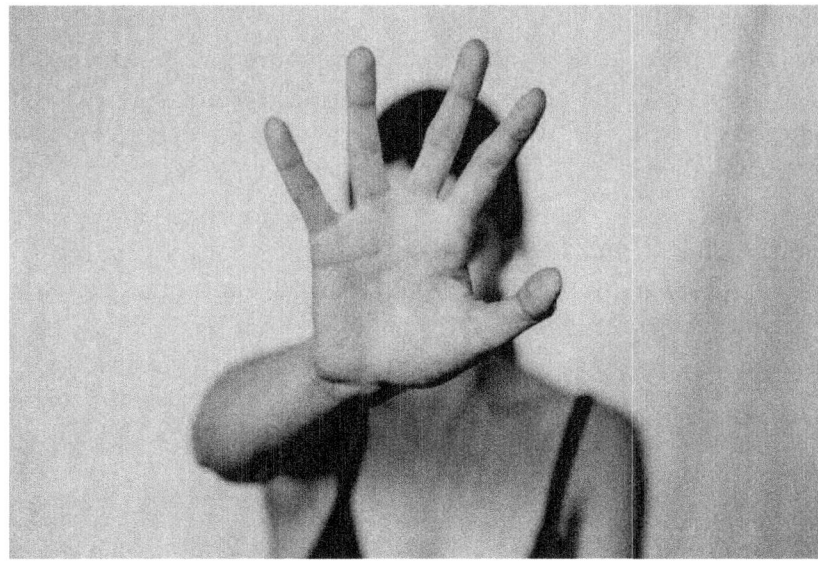

Setting boundaries is the first step towards healing from codependency.
https://www.pexels.com/photo/woman-showing-stop-gesture-with-hand-5723263/

Stop making others a priority and start focusing on *yourself*. Practice self-care by eating healthy, staying hydrated, meditating, exercising, and doing things you enjoy. Be strong and healthy, so even if someone you love leaves you, you will be fine because you will always have yourself.

Seek Supportive Relationships

Find people who love and support you and respect your boundaries. Healthy people teach you that you can feel safe in relationships and that not everyone will abandon you. Even if you don't have close friendships in your life, that's okay. Find someone you can trust and bond with, like an old friend or a family member. Surround yourself with positive people who encourage you to be yourself. Although this won't be easy for someone with a fear of abandonment, supportive people can make you feel accepted and validated.

Challenge Your Fear

Your fear isn't real, so don't treat it as if it's a *fact*! Challenge and question your thoughts and beliefs. For instance, if you believe that your partner is cheating, ask yourself for proof. What are you basing these claims on? Do you have evidence? If you do, is it rational and sure?

In most cases, you won't have any "proof". Even if you do, it will most likely be irrational, like they don't always answer your phone when you call them at work. Keep questioning and interrogating your thoughts until you get to the truth.

Stop looking at your loved ones as temporary people who will leave one day. Focus on the positive aspects of your relationships, like all the good things they do for you, how they make your life better, and all their good qualities.

Your past doesn't define you; it is only a chapter of your life. You can move on from it and heal in time – just focus on getting better and making yourself a priority. Don't listen to your fear; remember, you are strong, intelligent, amazing, and deserve to be loved.

Section 3: The Cost of Seeking Approval

There is nothing wrong with asking for other people's opinions or doing them a favor by obliging them from time to time. The problem comes when you find yourself wondering when the last time you did something you enjoyed was, or just because you felt like it and not because you thought someone would approve of it. After a while, you find yourself living someone else's life instead of your own. You look, speak, act, and think the way they do. You adopt their values, and everything that made you unique fades in the background. Unfortunately, this endless approval-seeking is a well-known trait of codependent people.

Feeling that you always need someone's approval to do or enjoy something is a form of codependence, the need for constant validation.

https://www.pexels.com/photo/a-grandmother-doing-online-shopping-5704398/

This chapter discusses the possible origins of this behavior, shedding light on the whys of the compulsive need for external validation. Besides a psychological analysis of this behavior, you'll also read about the costs and the importance of recognizing and addressing these issues for personal growth and healthier relationships. This chapter offers tips and practical activities to help you identify approval-seeking behavior and thought patterns and eliminate them from your life.

Why Do People Seek Approval?

Codependency has many possible origins — from family dynamics in early childhood and parenting styles to attachment styles to trauma and so much more. Early experiences become learned patterns, giving a person a distorted view of reality. How you view yourself and others over a long period of life can affect your behavior much later after this period is over. For example, suppose you subconsciously learned how to cope with difficult emotions by avoiding them, overcompensating, or healing with normalized yet misguided behaviors. In that case, you'll continue applying these behaviors whether or not the experience that led to these behaviors is still present.

In essence, by adopting certain approval-seeking techniques, you're following an unhealthy thought pattern modeled by your makeshift coping mechanism. While wanting other people's approval doesn't necessarily have to lead to codependency, it often does.

Family Dynamics

Family dynamics have a significant influence on people's perceptions of childhood. What you see in your family determines the way you perceive yourself in the world. Codependent thoughts can often take root from an early age, stemming from an unhealthy family system. For example, suppose a parent is either fully or partially absent from their child's life. In that case, the child can adopt approval seeking to ensure they won't be abandoned again.

Likewise, if a child is subjected to constant criticism by their parents and is only met with approval when they act and express values the parents agree with, they grow up suppressing their own needs and values. This child won't learn how to cope with their emotions healthily because they won't have had a chance to express themselves.

Unresolved conflicts between family members may lead to low self-esteem and seeking out codependent relationships later in life.

Attachment Styles

People's attachment styles play a prominent role in the rise of codependent thoughts and behaviors. Everyone has a slightly different approach to forming a relationship, which is essentially their attachment style. Part of this process is developing a mutually convenient and agreeable bond, at least in theory.

People who have other codependent traits (like fear of abandonment, for example) or traumatic experiences related to relationships will repeat the unhealthy coping mechanism. Then, they'll carry these into subsequent relationships. For instance, in romantic relationships, seeking approval is often viewed as cute and romantic, but it is often quite the opposite. While a partner could marvel at how selfless the other person is by always requiring their validation, sooner or later, they realize that this isn't good for a relationship.

Just as it can kill the most passionate romance, approval-seeking can also extinguish affection in any other form of relationship. It's learned and reinforced by an environment that teaches people that their worth comes from someone else, leading to neglecting their wants, needs, and boundaries.

Experiences of Abuse

Abuse is a particularly heinous form of trauma. It comes with overwhelming feelings of fear, shame, and powerlessness, which can cause codependent thoughts to form in the victim's mind. These emotions may manifest as low self-confidence, which, in turn, makes them turn to relationships where abuse and other inappropriate behaviors are considered normal.

Those who experience abuse often have trouble speaking up for themselves, neglecting their own needs just to avoid feeling bad. For them, the lines between healthy and unhealthy attachment are blurred, so they don't know how to advocate for their own needs when they feel controlled by another person.

These behaviors can become even more ingrained in individuals who have suffered long-lasting abuse. Without support from family, friends, and professionals, abuse survivors often find it impossible to break the cycle of codependency.

Fear of Rejection

Fear of rejection is also something children learn early in life. If they feel rejected for any reason, they'll do everything to keep those around them happy because they want to be loved and accepted. That is another example of identifying other people's approval as a good source of validation. Because they encounter more negative stimuli that make them feel rejected than positive ones that would cause them to find acceptance from within, they simply internalize the idea that the only way to feel safe is if others accept them. In their minds, pleasing those around them is the best way to achieve this.

Unhealthy Socialization Patterns

Socialization patterns are created by early experiences, which shape the person's values, beliefs, and ability to form a healthy connection with themselves and others. They vary from one culture to another and can lead to codependent thoughts.

Unhealthy socialization often leads to intense emotional attachment to another person, which is a hallmark trait of codependent people. Putting so much emphasis on external validation instead of finding approval within themselves can be learned at an early age. For example, women who grow up in households that rely heavily on traditional values may develop the belief that relationships must be sustained through subordination, which can often manifest into codependent behavior. They'll do everything to make their partner happy while subjecting themselves to a life devoid of joy and fulfillment.

Other improper socialization styles, such as constant criticism or someone's unwillingness to participate in meaningful conversations, can also contribute to codependent trait development.

Unfulfilled Needs

The origin of codependent thoughts can involve unmet needs. Your sense of worth can be questioned when you feel unheard, almost invisible to those around you. That can lead to a pattern of seeking validation or attention from others. Wanting to accommodate others can give you a sense of purpose and security, leading you to ignore your own well-being. Eventually, this becomes an unhealthy cycle of people-pleasing with an ever-increasing list of unmet needs in your own life.

Past Trauma

It's natural to want to support the people you love and care about, but feeling obligated and responsible for someone else's emotions, possessions, relationships, and life is entirely different. This destructive and unhealthy pattern of codependent thinking has its origins in childhood trauma. For example, a child growing up with alcoholic or neglectful parents and younger siblings will feel that they must take care of their siblings (and possibly even their parents), putting their own needs aside. That teaches them their worth is tied to how well they care for someone else. They will carry these unhealthy beliefs into adulthood, continuing the cycle in their adult relationships. To create more healthy connections and heal from childhood wounds, it's crucial to recognize and understand the origins of your patterns. Otherwise, you will struggle to move forward with your life.

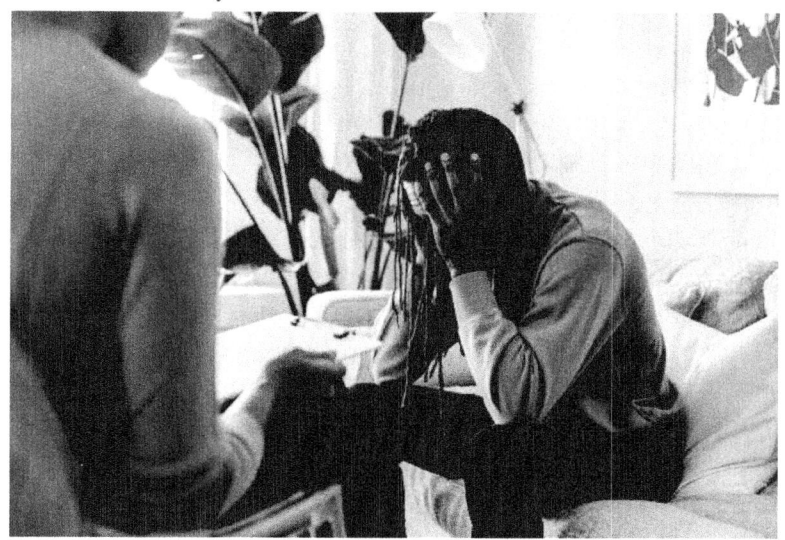

Past trauma stays and affects your perception and relationships if left untreated.

https://www.pexels.com/photo/stressed-black-man-with-dreadlocks-in-psychological-office-5699455/

A Biological Need for Approval

Beyond learned experiences, approval-seeking can also stem from people's innate need to base their happiness on social approval. This biological drive has existed since prehistoric times when people's survival depended on whether they kept each other out of harm's way.

Neuroscientists have found that several brain regions activate when a person isn't focusing on a specific task. These areas, known as the default network, are also found to be active when people navigate social situations, indicating that they're constantly monitoring their interactions with others, even if unintentionally.

The area lights up even in newborn babies' brains, revealing that social cognition is deeply rooted in people's biology. Still, this doesn't mean that people are driven to let go of their wants and needs and live the lives of others.

Scientists have also found that the default networks are only responsible for the need for positive social interactions. These can be achieved even if people satisfy their needs when navigating social situations. No one is driven to do this by seeking conditional approval from others. If they do, it is because they've developed codependent thoughts on top of the natural social cognition patterns.

The True Cost

While some could say that a bit of sacrifice can only strengthen a relationship, the true cost of approval-seeking goes beyond giving up one's own wants and needs. Relying on the approval or recognition of others can be downright dangerous for a person's emotional and mental health.

What would you think of a life where you would never be able to feel fulfilled or content without validation or attention from external sources, including family, friends, peers, or strangers? It doesn't sound appealing, right? Given that it leads to unhealthy relationship dynamics and loss of self-worth while feeling dominated, it isn't something anyone aspires to.

The problem is, when codependency starts rearing its ugly head, it happens almost unnoticeably. At first, you don't even realize the toll that depending on someone else takes on you. You'll then start feeling uncomfortable in your social interaction with others and focus your entire energy on pleasing and accommodating everyone around you instead of taking care of yourself.

It's normal to doubt your abilities. If someone else is there to affirm that you're doing a good job, you get an instant confidence boost. That's a lot like an employee on the first day of the job when they're complimented for handling a task efficiently.

Suppose you're struggling with self-esteem issues or self-doubt. In that case, external validation can also help you see yourself in a more positive light and remind you that you are capable of much more.

Positive affection from others also helps you feel more connected to and supported by them, which deepens your relationships. This will particularly appease those who previously felt isolated or lonely.

Approval-seeking behavior can even feel comforting at first. For example, if someone compliments your new outfit, you'll feel good about yourself and your choice of clothes. The same applies to social media approval. The more likes you get on that post, the better, no? Well, unfortunately, the feeling of accomplishment is very short-lived. Eventually, it will start hindering your growth and well-being.

Constantly needing the approval or recognition of others is one of the most prominent self-confidence killers. After all, if you learn to make decisions based on what others say, how can you possibly make a good one without external help?

When you keep receiving external validation, you're building a safety bubble around yourself. Stepping out of this very comfy zone will seem scary, and you'll be reluctant to do it. You will never venture into new waters to bring innovation into any area of your life because you'll be unwilling to take a risk.

While your need for external validation will only grow, this doesn't mean others will continue to oblige you in this. When the approval and recognition are delayed or don't come at all, no matter how hard you work on getting it, this leads to anxiety. Your emotional well-being becomes conditional on getting approved. Your self-esteem will already be in pieces, and worrying about whether you'll gain the much-awaited recognition will make things worse.

You can't always rely on validation from others to boost your self-esteem, just as you can't look at others to determine your self-worth. Yet, this is exactly the dangerous game codependent people are playing.

Low self-esteem often results in people pleasing, which is another codependent trait. When you place too much importance on what others think, your own wants and needs are pushed to the side, which can be detrimental to your relationships and your mental health.

External validation can lead to addiction. The more you seek those positive feelings when you get someone's approval, the more you crave them. Craving them will make you seek them out even more, but you won't always get them, which leads to disappointment and a tremendous amount of anxiety.

Worst of all, the validation you gain from external sources won't always be accurate. Social media is one of the best examples of this. Receiving likes from tons of people you don't know doesn't mean you're doing something right. Likewise, just because someone says you aren't good at something, this doesn't make it true.

However, if you believe it and stop doing it, you'll never learn whether you were genuinely incompetent or perhaps you could have done something to improve yourself. Living other people's lives will keep you from developing your skills and growing into the best version of yourself. Instead of pursuing your own goals, you follow the expectations of others, sacrificing your desires and happiness.

Introspective Exercise for Revealing Approval-Seeking Patterns

As a codependent person, you've most likely stopped paying attention to your own needs. This introspective exercise is based on a meditative practice that allows you to be alone with your thoughts. Using it, you'll be forced to reconnect with your intuition. Here is how to do this mediation:

1. Start by getting into a comfortable, relaxed position. You can sit, stand, or lie down.
2. Keep to your regular breathing and let it anchor you.
3. Close your eyes and focus on the sensations you experience in your body and mind. Notice any thoughts, feelings, sounds, images, smells, or anything else you may perceive.
4. Just be aware of what you feel, but don't try to investigate where the sensations come from.
5. Hone in on your thoughts and feelings. Are they different from the ones you get when you interact with others? How do they differ?
6. Think about the times you experience negative thoughts and feelings. Are there any specific situations when they appear? Do you get anxious when talking to a specific person, worrying whether they'll approve of what you say or do during the conversation?
7. Try going over as many details as possible about these situations, as this can help you see approval-seeking patterns emerge.

8. Alternatively, you can create a list of situations where your actions were driven more by the craving for approval than by your needs and wants.

_____
_____
_____
_____
_____
_____
_____
_____

Journaling

Keeping a journal is another way to force yourself to be more mindful of your thoughts and behavior in a codependent relationship. You can use it to write about your personal history and experiences, which may have led to your approval-seeking behavior.

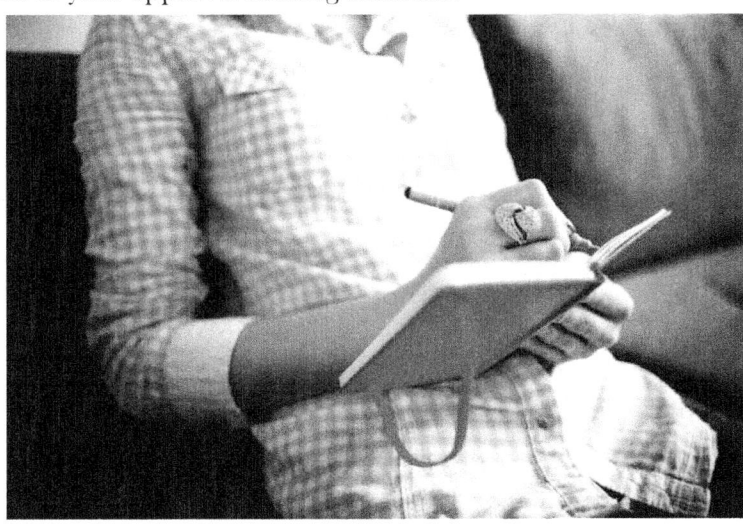

Journaling allows you to become more self-aware of your thoughts and patterns.
https://www.pexels.com/photo/person-writing-on-red-notebook-261735/

Here are a few tips for a successful journaling experience:

- **Journal in the Evening:** When you're getting ready for bed, go through the experiences you had during the day. Your mind will likely wander there naturally, so why not take advantage of this for some reflection time?
- **Don't Get Distracted:** Journaling requires focus, so make sure you remove any distractions like your phone, TV, or pets. If you don't live alone, ask the other household members to give you a little alone time.
- **Relax When Focusing on Stressful Situations:** Sometimes, this is easier said than done because stressful times inherently make relaxing challenging. However, by calming yourself, it will be much easier to pinpoint when you did something that went against your values and just to appease someone else. Codependency makes people do these unconsciously, so you'll need all the focus you can muster.
- **Revise Your Journal:** Review your entries at the end of each week and month. Notice any patterns in your thoughts, feelings, and behaviors when interacting with others. By uncovering these issues, you're enabling yourself to deal with them - instead of keeping them hidden behind codependent thoughts.

Self-Affirmation Practice

Another way to shift focus from external validation to internal self-acceptance and empowerment is by affirming your part in your positive experiences. It's also a great way to express gratitude for all the cheerful feelings you generate for yourself.

Instructions:

1. Think about what you feel grateful for about yourself. Create a list, focusing on anything you do that makes you happy. Omit everything that has to do with others.

_____

_____

_____

_____

2. Review your list, and consider why you've put each item on this list.
3. Focus on what you've achieved without other people's contribution. Are there more items on the list than you thought there would be?
4. As you do this exercise, you'll soon find plenty of things to be grateful for, allowing you to see that you can achieve a lot without needing anyone else's approval.
5. Now, come up with positive affirmations based on your achievements. You can make a list down below:

_____

_____

_____

_____

6. Once you have your list, identify the situations when you might need to use them. For example, when you suddenly feel the urge to seek someone's approval for a decision you're about to make. Here, you can reassure yourself that you're more than capable of making that decision on your own.
7. Pay attention to the ones that calm your mind and reduce your anxiety. These are the ones that chase away the worries and need for approval.
8. Keep the list with you so you can use it anytime a similar situation arises. When it does, you'll have your empowering affirmations on hand.

Going from constantly seeking others' approval to becoming confident in your ability to validate your thoughts, feelings, and actions is a long and eventful journey. It's a road full of ups and downs, but in the end, seeing yourself transformed into a strong, independent individual will be worth all the time and effort you put into it.

Looking inward for validation will bring much-needed positive changes, ultimately enabling you to build a meaningful and fulfilling life. It will be challenging at times, but every time you encounter a roadblock, just remember that no one else can make better decisions about your life better than you. No one can tell you whether something aligns with your values. Only you can do it. So why would you leave your entire source of happiness in the hands of others when you can shape it the best?

Section 4: Recognizing and Rectifying Self-Neglect

One of the key identifiers of codependency is self-neglect. Consistently diminishing your needs to uplift the needs of others is self-destructive and will result in the relationship becoming toxic. Taking care of your needs is not selfish because it puts you in a better position to help others while maintaining your mental, emotional, and physical health. The main issue with putting your needs on the back burner is that it invites manipulative and exploitative behavior. You should teach people how to treat you. You can't expect people to know where the line is if you don't set boundaries. You may not be the center of the universe, but you should be the center and the main character in your life.

Self-neglect can be extremely draining.
https://www.pexels.com/photo/grayscale-photo-of-a-person-hugging-self-7091503/

Self-neglect is not sustainable because you will become drained if you keep giving without receiving. Your primary caregiver is yourself. When you treat yourself well, you know exactly how others should treat you. You must build from the inside out to truly transform out of the codependent habits you have called home for so long. Becoming your main focus is one of the first steps to recovery. You are precious and worth more than you can imagine, so it is time for you to start treating yourself that way. Escaping from the clutches of self-neglect is genuinely liberating. It takes time to relearn your importance by understanding how self-neglect manifests, the factors that lead to it, and how you can begin resolving the trauma that creates it. Through the following healing protocols, you will recognize that you are worthy of the most profound love you can experience from yourself.

Neglecting Your Needs and Well-Being

When you put off thinking about yourself due to putting others first, it can be challenging to identify your own needs and make decisions to take care of your well-being. Self-neglect presents itself in multiple avenues of your life, including your appearance, nutrition, and behavior. You may find someone looking unkempt with dirty clothing or an untidy environment around them. Self-neglect can also present itself as a person starving or overeating. People who are neglecting themselves have no concern for their own health, so they could exhibit behavior like avoiding going to the doctor or not getting refills of chronic medication. Another sign of self-neglect could be mental health issues like depression, forgetfulness, confusion, and even psychosis.

When you neglect yourself, you don't pay attention to any of those negative expressions occurring in your life. You ignore them often to focus on the well-being of others while your health consistently deteriorates. The negative manifestations of self-neglect can also push healthy relationships away, especially if you tend to isolate yourself. Self-neglect becomes a vicious cycle as you fall deeper down into the void of suppressing your needs and desires while you push away those who can help pull you out of it. Self-neglect is an avenue to form codependent relationships with manipulative bloodsuckers who will allow and encourage your degradation. You need introspection and self-awareness to identify your needs and see the internal barriers standing in the way of fulfilling what you require before you serve others, especially those taking advantage of your imbalances.

Factors Leading to Self-neglect

Self-neglect is usually an intersection of multiple forces. It happens gradually as people fall deeper into low self-esteem, a fear of being selfish, and obsessive relationships that typically result from a fear of abandonment. A codependent relationship is not based on emotional support but on when the people involved believe that they cannot exist without one another. Therefore, your identity is tied to an individual in an unhealthy way. When you lose your identity to codependency, you get lost in the needs of the person you are in a relationship with. When you see your needs as the same as your codependent partner's needs, you are subject to neglecting your needs because you have blurred the lines of separation.

Low self-esteem, fearing being selfish, and abandonment issues are all linked to not having enough strength in your individuality. Humans are social, so people define themselves in a group or have relational identities. However, even within these relationships, it is crucial to assert your individuality so that you can become anchored in how you feel you should be treated. Throwing your needs away for others is the beginning of self-neglect because if you do not care about yourself, it is likely that others will walk all over you. Recovering from codependency requires you to reestablish the bond with yourself, so self-neglect is a big barrier to that essential internal relationship. Demanding the fulfillment of your needs from yourself is a hurdle you must cross to get through the desert of self-neglect.

Low Self-Esteem

Feeling like you are worthless and don't deserve love is a defining characteristic of low self-esteem. If you do not believe you are worthy of love, it logically follows that you will treat yourself in a way that reflects that attitude. The reason you enter a codependent relationship in the first place is that you are seeking external validation for the void created by your low self-esteem. When you've constantly been treated like you do not matter, you start to believe it and develop a negative opinion about yourself. When your opinion and perception of yourself are in the gutter, your actions start to reflect that, so you will not treat yourself in a way that maintains your mental and physical health.

Low self-esteem destroys your ability to grow and affects your relationships.
https://www.pexels.com/photo/woman-standing-in-front-of-brown-wood-plank-1458826/

In the codependent dynamic, you get your validation from the relationship. Catering to all the other party's needs feels like loving yourself. The temporary treatment for your low self-esteem is the misdirected fulfillment you feel in a codependent relationship. You attempt to prove your worth by how much you give, but your self-neglect breaks you down so much that you feel even more worthless. The more you pour from an empty cup, the more incapable you become of giving. Escaping the codependency and low self-esteem trap requires the realization that you control your perception of yourself. Your worth does not lie in someone's opinion of you but in your intrinsic value as a person. Once you internalize and fully accept that you deserve love, you will slowly stop neglecting yourself.

Fear of Selfishness

Taking care of yourself is not selfish. When you define your worth on what you can give in a relationship, a break from giving can feel self-centered. Breaking from self-neglect requires you to realize that having your own desires, hopes, and ambitions is okay. Not everything you desire must align with the people around you. Friends and partners often have common goals and values that attract them to one another. However, these shared interests do not mean that every aspect of your personality will align. Codependency often results in you adopting your partner's desires as if they were your own. When there is a split in desires, and you cannot fulfill the requirement, you continue to do what does not align with your values because of a fear of being perceived as selfish.

There is a time to be selfish. You cannot keep giving without receiving. Eventually, your desires are placed last when you give everything you have. Sometimes, being selfish helps you hold on to the core of your being without getting lost in co-dependency. The problem with being completely unselfish is that you become the meal ticket for selfish people. You attract vampiric personalities when you present yourself on a platter as a free meal. They have no problem draining you because they have no regard for your well-being. You cannot allow yourself to slip too far into the spectrum of unselfishness because, at some point, extreme self-sacrifice for the sake of others turns into self-destructive martyrdom.

Being Overly Focused on Others

Focusing on others too much ties into a fear of selfishness. If your mind is always on somebody else, you never get the opportunity to think about yourself. This results in neglecting your needs because you are not giving them attention. It is noble to work in the service of others and to be generous, but it should never be at the cost of your health. Think of how you treat other people and your desires for their lives. Imagine what you would do to help them get to that mountain top. Now, ask yourself why you do not do those things for yourself. Being overly focused on others means that your own well-being never even occurs to you.

Constantly taking your attention off yourself to put it on to others is also an avoidance tactic to get away from facing your own trauma. When you focus on others all the time, you do not have to do the introspective work to address the voids you face. Codependency is a way to bypass your own trauma. The easiest way to avoid looking at the dark, difficult places where you need healing is to focus on trying to "fix" the people around you. To identify the reasons you embrace codependent relationship structures, you must find the sources that motivate you to head in that direction. By focusing on others, you never attain the introspection needed to work on your own emotional and psychological well-being.

Consequences of Prolonged Self-neglect

Prolonged self-neglect can spiral into more serious issues, including depression, hoarding, and a rapid deterioration of mental and physical health. Quite often, when people are deep into self-neglect, they will decline any help they are offered. This is why a one-sided codependent relationship can be a place of comfort for an individual who is not looking after themselves. Therefore, when you decide to begin recovery from a codependent relationship, be open to people helping you within boundaries with which you are comfortable.

You can create a regular self-care schedule to reduce the possibility of long-term self-neglect. Start slowly, and work your way up to more significant changes. For example, if you have neglected your physical appearance by wearing dirty or torn clothes, buy a new outfit every month. You do not have to break your budget because there are many affordable options. Even something as simple as getting your hair styled can pave the way for you to stop embracing self-neglect. The guilt attached to self-care and relating it to self-indulgence holds you back from maintaining your internal world, which, with time, will be reflected in your environment and appearance. A simple way to start caring for yourself is to clean and tidy the space around you. Before you can conquer the world's big challenges, grow from the central space where you are most comfortable by cleaning your room, office, or sitting area.

Burnout

Burnout is a drastic collapse of your physical and mental health. Think of yourself as a car. You can miss a few services, and the vehicle will still keep moving. Eventually, you'll hear weird sounds, cracks, and clunks, but you can still ignore them and keep driving. Soon, your car will start struggling to start or even break down. You can then do a few quick fixes to get it moving again, but inevitably, a day will come when everything piles up, and your trusted vehicle gives up on you. When you find yourself in a codependent relationship and are consistently suppressing your own needs to take care of your partner's or friend's desires, you will eventually get overwhelmed as the neglect becomes more apparent. Your body and mind will give you warning signs, and you will break down if you do not respond to them.

Imagine you had a child, and you completely ignored all their emotional needs by brushing off their desires as if they did not matter.

Eventually, the child would start acting up and become socially maladapted. This antisocial behavior can become exponentially worse, resulting in self-destructive tendencies. Essentially, you neglect the child within you when you do not provide yourself with the necessary love, care, and compassion. You will start demanding this attention from yourself in uncontrollable ways and eventually hit the brick wall of burnout as your mind and body's last-ditch attempt at getting you to maintain it.

Resentment

Constantly putting your own needs aside so you can fulfill the desires of others always leads to resentment, bitterness, and emptiness. Putting yourself in last place is not a sustainable way to live your life. The irony about neglecting your own needs for the benefit of someone else is that you will start blaming them for the emptiness you feel, even if they are not directly at fault. You will feel like you are owed something you never asked for. By neglecting yourself for the sake of others, you pour your resources into an investment that has no return. Resentment often leads to toxic passive-aggressiveness and terrible communication habits. When resentment gets into the picture, many of your relationships will break down because it will start showing in your behavior.

Resentment will show itself in numerous ways, like talking badly behind a person's back or becoming tense when they are around. You will start developing feelings of anger and disappointment as well. If you are still in a position of self-neglect and put the person's needs before yours, there could also be a level of guilt and shame for the negative emotions you feel. This resentment will cause a wedge in relationships, and even when you end a codependent relationship, if left unresolved, the resentment will continue to impact how you treat others. Resentment encourages you to hold grudges, create distance, and embrace an attitude of distrusting people. Before you start any new relationships, you should address your lingering resentment by forgiving and setting boundaries with your time and energy.

Diminished Sense of Self

In a codependent relationship where you center the needs of the next person before your own, your sense of self could get lost as you take on the identity of your partner or get defined by the relationship. You may find yourself doing things that are not like you at all or being uncertain about what your needs are. When you lose your sense of self, you become more susceptible to manipulation and exploitation because anybody can fill the gap of your identity with their desires. Staying grounded in who you are and what you value is important. To do that:

1. Write down your values.
2. Write down your priorities.
3. Using a minimum of 500 words, write down your ideal life. Include your physical, mental, emotional, and financial ideals.
4. What steps will you take to create this life?
5. What boundaries do you need to establish to make sure no one prevents you from pursuing your ideal life?
6. Describe how you believe others see you.
7. Describe how you see yourself.
8. What are the differences between how you see yourself and how you believe others see you, and why do these differences exist?

Mindfulness Meditation Exercise

To break free from self-neglect and to re-establish the broken bond with yourself, you must understand what your needs, values, and desires are. This requires introspective meditation so you can explore and navigate the mysterious darkness of yourself from which you have disconnected.

Mindful meditation can be done at any time to help you reconnect with yourself.
https://www.pexels.com/photo/woman-meditating-in-bedroom-3772612/

Try this reflective meditation:

1. Find a quiet space where you will not be disturbed. A dark or dimly lit room will work best.
2. Lie down flat on your back or sit up with your spine erect.
3. Relax and inhale deeply as you count to ten. Then, take a deep breath out, counting to ten as well. Breathe in through your nostrils and out through your mouth. Stay focused on your breath. Whenever your mind starts to wander, bring your attention back to your breath. Repeat this cycle until you feel relaxed and at ease.
4. Now, breathe more naturally and allow your thoughts to flow in and out of your mind without any judgment. You'll notice that after a while, your thoughts will begin looping and repeating a similar cycle. This is when you are ready for the next step.
5. Take a few more deep breaths and notice any discomfort or negative emotions that you are feeling.
6. Visualize a large treasure chest in the middle of a huge, empty, black room.
7. As you continue taking deep breaths in and out, imagine the negative feelings and discomfort you feel filling up the treasure chest.
8. Slowly walk toward the treasure chest, as it continues filling up with these negative emotions and discomfort.
9. You open the treasure chest to find a large crystal ball covered with black soot.
10. You dust off the soot as you continue to breathe. As you dust the soot, you feel the negative emotions leaving the room. Once the crystal ball is clear, you look inside it. In the crystal ball are the unfulfilled needs your negative emotions were covering.
11. What is the crystal ball showing you?
12. How have you neglected yourself for these needs to be unfulfilled?
13. What boundaries can you set to make sure that these needs are taken care of?
14. What self-care activities can fulfill these needs?

15. Now, in the distance, you see a bright light. As you continue focusing on your breath and your unfulfilled needs, walk into that light. As you walk, the actions you should take to fulfill your needs become clearer.
16. As you step into the light, you feel relief from all the leftover negative emotions leaving your body. Inhale deeply to breathe in all the positivity, and exhale to breathe out all the negativity before slowly opening your eyes.

How do you feel?

Daily Self-Care Checklist

Go through this list every day to see if you are meeting your self-care requirements. Feel free to personalize the checklist and add needs that are unique to you.

Physical Self-Care
- Did you have three balanced meals today?
- Did you exercise for thirty minutes?
- Did you get enough sleep?
- Did you go outside?
- If you're on medication, did you take them?

Psychological Self-Care
- Did you take time off from screens?
- Did you rest?
- Did you take time to reflect on your own needs and desires?
- Did you say no to extra responsibilities?
- Did you try something new today?

Emotional Self-Care
- Did you talk to a loved one?
- Did you take the time to love yourself?
- Did you listen to music?
- Did you allow yourself to cry?
- Did you express yourself creatively?

Self-Care Contract

Formalizing an agreement with yourself to take care of your needs makes it clearer and more solidified in your mind. Complete the following contractual agreement to center your needs so you can take the necessary steps to fulfill your self-care requirements and prevent self-neglect. You can even have a hard copy of this contract and put it in a visible place to always be reminded of the commitment you made to take care of yourself. You should renew this contract after three months because your needs may have evolved, so your self-care requirements will shift. Fill in the following contractual agreement:

This is a self-care, self-compassion, and self-love contract between (enter name) *and their essence.*

This agreement is a pledge to take care of my needs first before I use my loving drive to take care of the needs of others. I cannot pour from an empty cup, so this agreement is to ensure that (enter name) *always has a full cup so I can be a blessing to myself, those around me, and the extended community.*

I (enter name) *will take care of the following physical needs*

(List your physical needs)

By

(List the actions you will take to fulfill your physical daily needs)

I (enter name) *will take care of the following emotional needs*

(List your emotional daily needs)

By

(List the actions you will take to fulfill your emotional daily needs)

I (enter name) *will take care of the following mental needs*

(List your mental needs)

By

(List the actions you will take to fulfill your mental daily needs)

I (enter name) *will take care of the following spiritual needs*

(List your spiritual needs)

By

(List the actions you will take to fulfill your spiritual daily needs)

I pledge that I will fulfill all these needs and correct my path whenever I start embracing self-neglect. I also pledge to renew this contract every three months as my needs evolve so that I am updated with the actions I should take in my life to look after myself.

Date:

Signature:

Section 5: Boundaries and Codependency

Sometimes, setting and maintaining healthy boundaries in relationships becomes a continuous and overwhelming task. Yet, it's the most practical way to fight and overcome those fears of abandonment, people-pleasing habits, and self-neglect.

Defining these boundaries in relationships is necessary. Without them, getting lost in the whirlwind of emotions is easy, and chaos can take over. These boundaries create the foundation for healthy connections without losing yourself.

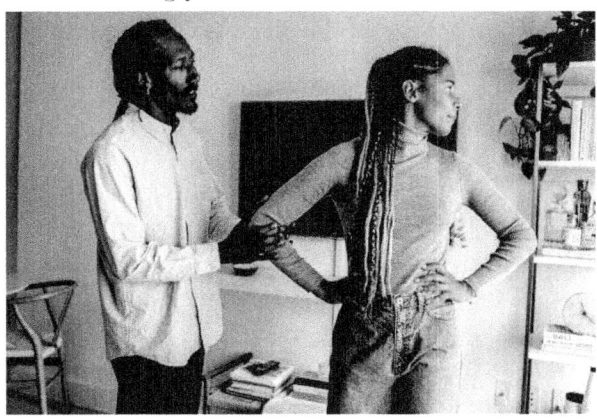

It's not easy to set boundaries in relationships, but in the long run, this is what strengthens the bond.

https://www.pexels.com/photo/black-woman-taking-offense-of-boyfriend-5699850/

In this chapter, you will explore why boundaries are your lifeline in codependency recovery, dig into practical strategies, and read about actionable steps to build boundaries in your relationships.

Codependency in Relationships

In codependent relationships, the lines that traditionally separate identities become blurred, creating a shared canvas where the emotions, desires, and fears of both people come in. There's nothing wrong with being flexible in codependent relationships. The threads of your existence seamlessly merge with those around you, but in some cases, these poor boundaries take a toll on your well-being. This intermixing of emotions and experiences in codependent relationships is no less than navigating through a dense fog. The boundaries that differentiate your feelings from your partner's become obscured, making it challenging to discern whose emotions are whose. In this foggy landscape, your once distinct and defined identity dissipates.

Challenges in Establishing Boundaries

Fear of Abandonment

This fear makes it hard to set boundaries when a partner is reluctant to create any distance that might trigger feelings of rejection or isolation. The desire for constant connection and reassurance can override the rational instinct to establish healthy limits. The need for approval and affirmation from others also becomes so ingrained that setting boundaries can jeopardize the very foundation of one's identity.

Here's a scenario to showcase this fear of being left alone in a codependent relationship:

Emma is a vibrant soul navigating a codependent relationship with determination. Still, her fear of rejection, deeply ingrained from past experiences, makes setting boundaries challenging. The mere thought of expressing her needs triggers a surge of emotions and anxiety, as she fears that asserting herself might lead to disputes and even ending the relationship. In her mind, the risk of rejection outweighs the potential benefits of establishing clear boundaries.

Guilt and Obligation

The codependent person often carries a heavy emotional burden of guilt and obligation. This sense of responsibility arises as an obstacle to boundary-setting, as the fear of disappointing or hurting the partner overrides the need for personal space. The emotional shackles of guilt become a roadblock to asserting one's needs through establishing clear boundaries.

Here is another scenario:

A young, warm-hearted man named James yearns for a connection but is plagued by a lack of assertiveness. In codependent relationships, James finds it challenging to communicate his limits without fearing conflict or displeasure. He remains silent when faced with a situation that clashes with his preferences. The fear of rocking the boat or causing discomfort stifles his ability to express his needs assertively, perpetuating the cycle of codependency.

Becoming the Mirror

The expectations and desires of your partner become crucial goals to achieve, and people-pleasing tendencies take center stage in attempts to seek validation and acceptance. This constant struggle leads to a continuous adaptation of oneself to meet the perceived needs of the other. The adaptive behavior further blurs the lines of individuality, as personal desires and aspirations are overshadowed by the relentless pursuit of pleasing your partner.

Jane and James have been in a romantic relationship for a few years. Jane tends to be the people-pleaser in the relationship, prioritizing James's needs and wishes over her own. On the other hand, James understands this dynamic and often takes advantage of Jane's willingness to please.

This people-pleasing attitude consistently portrayed by Jane affects several aspects of their codependent relationship. Here are some of the aspects:

Communication

Jane receives a last-minute invitation to a social gathering with her friends. Still, James expresses disappointment, hoping they could spend the evening together. Hearing her partner's decision, Jane decides to cancel her plans with friends to be with James, even though she was looking forward to the gathering.

Decision-Making

James plans to move out to a new city and find work there. Jane has reservations but hesitates to express her concerns, fearing it may upset him. Following her people-pleasing behavior, Jane suppresses her concerns and agrees with James's decision, even if it goes against her goals and desires.

Personal Boundaries

James often requests financial support from Jane, even though it strains her budget and causes her stress. Still, she continues with her people-pleasing behavior, providing financial assistance while compromising her own financial stability.

In all these different settings, Jane's people-pleasing behavior reinforces the codependent dynamic. She prioritizes James's needs and wishes, neglecting her own well-being and compromising boundaries. Over time, this pattern leads to resentment, emotional exhaustion, and an unhealthy power imbalance in the relationship. Breaking free from patterns like these requires establishing clear communication, setting boundaries, and prioritizing one's needs for a healthier relationship.

Self-Neglect

Without clear boundaries, self-neglect gradually starts affecting your individual needs. This consistent surge of self-neglect is similar to the relentless waves washing away the shoreline. Personal aspirations and desires slowly fade into the background.

Alex is a kind-hearted individual with lots of love to offer. However, deep-seated feelings of low self-worth undermine his ability or will to set boundaries. He questions the validity of his personal needs, convinced they are not as significant as those of others. He has already developed a perspective that asserting boundaries is an audacious act reserved for those with a higher, more deserving status. Alex consistently sacrifices personal time and preferences to meet the expectations of others. The subtle belief that his own needs are secondary diminishes the chances of defining boundaries that could nurture a healthier sense of self.

Lack of Role Models

For many people grappling with codependency, the absence of healthy boundary-setting role models in the early years creates problems in setting boundaries. If someone doesn't know or has yet to witness a role model setting clear boundaries in relationships, the skillset required to establish and maintain them becomes very difficult. Breaking the cycle requires learning the concept of healthy boundaries and the healthy ways these boundaries should be implemented.

The difficulty in establishing boundaries in codependent relationships has many causes, which include fears, ingrained behavioral patterns, and emotional complexities. Recognizing these hurdles is the first step toward understanding and compassion. In the subsequent sections, you will read about navigating these challenges through strategies so you can pave the path toward healthier, more boundary-conscious relationships.

The boundaries you will be setting are like fine threads that can be used to shape and give direction in relationships. These boundaries aren't barriers but a roadmap that defines the unique colors of each individual. It will shape your shared space, ensuring that each person maintains their distinct identity while contributing to the richness of the collective experience. Furthermore, you'll be giving structure and harmony to the relationship. They are a guideline allowing the expression of individual needs and desires.

Navigating the complexities of your codependent relationships can be made easy with boundaries as they redefine and enhance the beauty of shared and individual elements. Embrace the journey of untangling, setting clear boundaries, and appreciating the nuanced artistry of connection.

Activity: Boundary-Setting Scriptwriting Workshop

Scriptwriting teaches you assertiveness skills through reflection.
https://www.pexels.com/photo/woman-checking-the-script-written-on-the-paper-8085944/

Objective: Develop assertiveness skills through practical scriptwriting

What You Need:
- Pen and paper or a note app
- A quiet and comfortable space for reflection
- Clear mind and the willingness to engage

Instructions:

Step 1: Setting the Stage

Begin by creating a comfortable and quiet space for reflection. Take a few deep breaths to center yourself and promote a sense of openness to the process. Sink into the peaceful surroundings and free your mind from clouding thoughts. Now, shift your focus and start reflecting on setting boundaries.

Step 2: Identify Scenarios

Think of scenarios in your life where setting boundaries is necessary. These could include situations at work, with family, friends, or romantic partners. Consider both past situations and potential future scenarios where there could be a need to set healthy boundaries.

Step 3: Be the Protagonist

Play the role of a protagonist in each scenario. Develop your character by considering your values, emotions, and desired outcomes. Be honest about your feelings and needs in each situation. The more openly you get involved, the easier the path toward promoting assertiveness within yourself becomes. At the end of this practice, you'll have a complete roadmap of the boundaries you must set.

Step 4: Scriptwriting

Start writing scripts for each scenario, focusing on assertive communication to express your boundaries. Be specific, and use "I" statements to convey your feelings and needs. Consider potential responses and reactions from others, and incorporate assertive responses. You should also anticipate the possible reactions and responses from others that you will get.

Example Script

Scenario: A co-worker consistently interrupts your work to discuss non-urgent matters.

Your Line:

I appreciate these interactions, but I've noticed that I'm often interrupted while working on essential tasks. I'd like to set specific times for discussions or catch-ups to be more productive. How does that sound to you?

Anticipated Response:

Your co-worker may express surprise, disagreement, or agree to the suggestion.

Step 5: Refine

After writing each script, reflect on how asserting yourself in those hypothetical situations felt. Note any emotional challenges or reservations during the exercise and try resolving them so you have no issues implementing these boundaries.

Step 6: Role-Play

If you feel comfortable, you can get the help of a friend or family member to engage in role-playing the scenarios. This adds an interactive element, allowing you to practice assertiveness in a supportive environment.

Step 7: Discuss

Share your experience and scripts with a trusted friend, family member, or within a support group. Discuss your gains, the challenges you faced, and strategies that can be implemented for improvement. You can ask them to be fair in their observation and take the feedback constructively.

Step 8: Apply

Use the feedback and insights gained from the activity to refine your scripts or create new ones. Apply these assertiveness skills in real-life situations, gradually building confidence in setting and maintaining healthy boundaries.

Remember, this exercise is a journey of self-discovery and growth. Each step taken in asserting your boundaries contributes to building healthier, more fulfilling relationships. It's possible that the boundaries can take time to be implemented, or you might even have to be flexible to achieve results similar to what you want.

Navigating the Emotional Terrain of Boundary-Setting

Setting boundaries is a courageous step towards reclaiming your sense of self in codependent relationships. However, this journey is not without its challenges and emotions. Guilt and potential pushback from others are some common hurdles that require a bit of navigation to maintain your newfound boundaries steadfastly.

Emotional Challenges

When setting boundaries for healthy codependent relationships, feelings of guilt can surface, especially when you are in self-neglect and prioritize others' needs over your own. You may fear letting someone down or being perceived as selfish when asserting your needs.

Remember that guilt is a natural response to change, especially when breaking ingrained patterns you have followed for some time. Acknowledge the feeling without judgment and remind yourself that prioritizing your own well-being is not selfish but necessary for healthy relationships. Reframe the narrative in your mind that you're not rejecting others but affirming yourself.

Internal Dialogues to Try

Sometimes, arguing with yourself and engaging in internal dialogues can resolve inner conflicts. Here is an example of an internal dialogue for reference:

"It's okay to prioritize my needs. There's nothing wrong in creating a space where I feel respected and fulfilled. This is not about rejecting others but about honoring my well-being."

Pushback from Others

Pushback or resistance should be anticipated when you assert your boundaries. When you face this resistance, it evokes anxiety or fear of conflict.

Response to Change

The pushback or resistance you face in codependent relationships is a natural response to change. Respect and validate the other person's emotions, but don't compromise your needs. Communicate assertively and empathetically, explaining the importance of your boundaries for your well-being. Here is an example script showing how a person should communicate about setting boundaries:

"I understand this change may be surprising, and I appreciate your perspective. However, I must set these boundaries for my growth and happiness. Please understand and support me in this."

Fear of Isolation

As mentioned earlier, the fear of being isolated, left out, or strained in relationships sometimes stops you from setting boundaries. While some adjustments may occur, remember that authentic connections are only built when mutual understanding and respect for each other's needs exist. Share your intentions with loved ones to alleviate their concerns and emphasize that your goal is to create healthier connections. Here's an example:

"I want to be honest about my journey in setting boundaries. It's not about distancing myself. It's about creating a more balanced and authentic connection with you. I value our relationship and hope we can navigate this together."

Nurturing Confidence

Doubting your right to set boundaries can undermine your confidence. You may question whether your needs are valid or if you're deserving of a healthier relationship dynamic. Remember that your needs are inherently valid, and you can prioritize your well-being. Seek support from friends, family, or a therapist who can affirm the importance of your journey.

Journaling can also be a powerful tool to reflect on your progress and reinforce your commitment to self-care. You can write about the positive changes you have noticed since setting boundaries and how those changes contributed to your well-being and sense of self-worth.

Navigating the emotional terrain of boundary-setting requires patience, self-compassion, and resilience. Embrace the discomfort as a sign of growth, knowing that prioritizing your needs contributes to healthier, more authentic connections. As you journey through these challenges, remember that you're not alone. Countless individuals have walked this path before you, fostering self-discovery and nurturing stronger, more fulfilling relationships. Keep the faith in your journey and celebrate each step toward a more empowered and authentic you.

Activity: Guided Visualization for Calm Assertiveness

Visualization allows you to calm your mind and focus on assertiveness.
https://www.pexels.com/photo/photo-of-a-man-sitting-near-the-window-846747/

Objective: Cultivate a state of calm and centered assertiveness in the face of resistance

What You Need:
- Comfortable and quiet space
- A chair or cushion for comfortable seating
- **Optional:** soothing background music or nature sounds if it doesn't distract you from visualizing

Instructions:

Find Your Sanctuary

Cut all communications with the outside world and sit comfortably in a quiet space without interruption. Take a few deep breaths, inhaling deeply through your nose and exhaling through your mouth. Close your eyes and release tension as you settle into your seat.

Grounding Breathwork

Inhale deeply, counting to four, allowing your chest and abdomen to expand fully. Hold your breath briefly, then exhale slowly to the count of six, releasing any tension or stress. Repeat this breath cycle several times until you feel a sense of relaxation. You can even try deep breathing exercises or meditate for a few minutes to clear the head.

Visualize Calm Waters

Visualize yourself standing at the edge of a tranquil lake surrounded by lush greenery. The water is clear and calm, reflecting the gentle sunlight. As you immerse yourself in the serene surroundings, recognize that this lake represents your inner calm. Float in the lake's calmness and try calming your inner self like the visualization.

Embrace Your Strength

Imagine a warm and vibrant energy emanating from your core, symbolizing your assertiveness. Visualize this energy flowing down your arms and into your hands. As you open your palms, feel a sense of empowerment and clarity radiating from your fingertips.

Boundary Assertion

Bring the person with whom you must assert your boundaries into the visualization, standing across the lake. As you express your needs assertively, visualize your words transforming into ripples that gracefully cross the water. These ripples represent the positive impact of your assertiveness on the relationship.

Resistance as Ripples

Anticipate potential resistance as small ripples on the lake's surface. Instead of disrupting your calm, see these ripples as natural reactions to change. Allow them to dissipate on the water, acknowledging that they don't diminish the strength of your assertiveness.

Affirm Your Boundaries

Inhale deeply, affirming to yourself that your boundaries are valid and essential for your well-being. Exhale any remaining tension, letting the calmness of the lake envelop you. Repeat positive affirmations like, "My needs are valid, and I deserve healthy boundaries."

Gratitude and Reflection

Slowly bring your awareness back to the present, acknowledging the strength within you. Express gratitude for this moment of self-reflection. When you're ready, open your eyes and carry this sense of calm assertiveness with you into your interactions.

Empowered Assertiveness

This guided visualization can be turned into a powerful tool to cultivate a state of calm assertiveness. As you face resistance to your boundaries, remember the serene lake within you, the strength it represents, and the incredible impact this journey holds for you.

Safeguarding Your Emotional Well-Being

Your boundaries are guardians of your emotional well-being, providing a haven for expressing your feelings, needs, and desires without fear. Prioritizing self-care strengthens your emotional resilience, paving the way for a more stable and fulfilling life. Staying emotionally sound also keeps any mental health issues like anxiety and depression at bay.

Reshaping Relationship Dynamics

Consider boundaries as both barriers and bridges. They act as barriers that protect you from toxicity, so your connections are grounded in mutual respect. Simultaneously, they are bridges that allow authentic communication and more meaningful connections.

Breaking Free from Codependency

Setting clear boundaries is pivotal in breaking free from the chains of codependency. It shifts the dynamic from enmeshment to autonomy. You'll have a chance to avoid practicing people-pleasing behaviors, stop fearing that your boundaries can end the codependent relationship, and not indulge in self-neglect behaviors again. These changes can create space for healthier patterns to emerge.

Promoting Growth

While you will try to assert boundaries, you must also deliver a fundamental message to invite others to devise their boundaries. This mutual respect can take a codependent relationship to new heights as both are willing and actively participate in implementing healthy boundaries.

Embracing Harmony

Your boundaries bring balance to the intricate dance of relationships. They ensure that burdens are shared, creating a harmonious exchange of support and understanding. You and the other person can flourish independently in this balanced dance while co-creating a shared connection.

As you internalize the importance of boundaries, remember that you sculpt a life filled with authenticity, resilience, and connections that nourish your soul. Take in the transformative power of healthy boundaries and let them be the bridges that lead you to deeper, more meaningful relationships. Throughout your journey, remember that it will take time, patience, and persistence to set these boundaries. Challenges and setbacks are evident. Still, it's crucial to strive hard and follow an action plan so you can achieve the set goal of creating, implementing, and maintaining healthy boundaries. This journey is uniquely yours, and every step you take will bring you closer to your end goal.

Section 6: Finding Yourself: The Journey to Self-Discovery

One of the downsides of codependency is losing your sense of self for the other person or people in your life. If you were in a relationship like this one, you must have found yourself putting other people's needs before yours more often than not. The sad thing is that instead of feeling satisfied and fulfilled for giving yourself and your time to someone, you often feel terrible. It's normal. You're not alone. Why does this happen? Sometimes, it's rooted in past experiences like family dynamics or unhealthy relationships. It could be a fear of abandonment, a need for approval, or a pattern you haven't questioned.

Self-discovery is found through a number of practices.
https://www.pexels.com/photo/portrait-photo-of-smiling-woman-in-red-long-sleeve-top-thinking-3768897/

The problem with codependency is that it's as if you're letting someone else jump in the driver's seat of your life. They might be well-meaning, but they take you to their destination, not yours. While you're busy navigating someone else's route, your dreams and talents will be pushed to the backseat. You may have phenomenal artistic skills, a knack for coding, or a burning desire to travel the world. But codependency leaves you feeling drained, lacking the energy and confidence to pursue your own skills.

It's not just about passions, though. Codependency can mess with your love life, too. You may attract partners who need "fixing" or end up in relationships where your needs are constantly ignored. Healthy love should feel like something other than a constant rescue mission.

Are you at a point in your life where you've realized that your choices, thoughts, actions, and style weren't yours? It's time to take back the steering wheel and find yourself. Self-discovery is one of the best things that can happen to a person battling codependency issues. Taking the first step is usually the hardest, but you're doing great. You tried this book, and you've read up to this point. That is progress. Finding yourself may seem like a scary feat now, something that can only be achieved further in the future. But that's not true. You can do it. Don't worry about how and where to start.

Why Do You Lose Yourself in Codependent Relationships?

Most problems are usually half solved when the cause is identified. Imagine for a moment you had a door that once used to lock properly when you closed it, and suddenly, it no longer does. Each time you want to lock it, you only manage to do so by forcing it. After some time, you decide to contact a professional who knows more about doors. After inspection, they will first tell you the issue before giving you solutions. That's how it is with codependency. You need first to understand why you seem to fall into relationships or tend to be codependent. That is the first step toward your self-discovery. Take a look at some of the common factors that contribute to self-loss in codependent relationships.

You're Always Putting Them First: Every time your best friend or partner is having a meltdown, you drop everything to comfort them and just be there for them instead of going out like you may have planned. This happens a lot in codependent relationships. Even if it means neglecting yourself, you'll still go out of your way to cater to their every need.

You Freak Out if They Leave: Say you make plans with your friend, but they never text you back to confirm or reassure you that they're all in. You keep wondering and stressing about what could be going on in your friend's head. Your mind is racing with possibilities. Is everything okay? Did something happen? Are they tired of you? Do they no longer want to be seen with you? What would you do if they were no longer your friend? You even go as far as stalking them online, and the moment you find out they have a new friend, your stomach turns. Jealousy and insecurity take over. Codependents often have a fear of being alone, which can make them clingy and lose sight of their own independence.

You Don't Know Where to Draw the Line: Your friend keeps making bad decisions, and all you want to do is swoop in to save the day. You absorb all their emotions when they tell you about something that got them upset. You're worried that they'll withdraw from you if you say "no" to your friend. What this does is smudge or make your boundaries non-existent. Boundaries are invisible lines that protect your space and feelings. Your thoughts and feelings belong to you, which is not always the case for people in codependent relationships. Codependents feel responsible for fixing other people's problems, even if they got themselves in the mess to begin with!

You Don't Have a Lot of Appreciation for Yourself: You find yourself caring so much about what they think of you. You keep comparing yourself to them. Codependents often struggle with confidence, which can make them settle for less in friendships and relationships. They are prone to forgetting their own dreams and goals along the way. They avoid conflict and disapproval at all costs. Even if it means downplaying their talents and ambitions to make sure the other person is the star of the show, they'll do it.

Codependents spend far too much of their precious lives caught up in someone else's drama, which they have no control over. The journey ahead may be a bit bumpy, but be patient with yourself. These things take time. You can break free and discover the amazing person you truly are. Here are some activities to help you do just that.

Activity 1: Create a Personal Timeline

Step 1: You're going to need a timeline. Grab a pen, some paper, or your favorite typing app. Picture your entire life as a timeline. Make it stretch from your earliest memories as a child to the present day. Take note of key events, turning points, and significant experiences that shaped you so far.

Answer These Questions:
- What were some major life changes you experienced (e.g., moving, family transitions, or personal achievements)?
- Were there any moments of loss, heartbreak, or challenge that had a lasting impact?
- What positive experiences stand out in your life?

Step 2: Reflect on the turning points you discovered. Then, select 3-5 key events from your timeline that feel the most impactful. For each one, answer these questions:
- What were the emotions and thoughts associated with this event?
- How did this experience influence your choices and behavior?
- What did you learn about yourself from this turning point?

Activity 2: Determine Your Values

Step 1: You can lie to everyone else *but never to yourself.* Think of the values and beliefs that really matter to you, and take a moment to reflect on them. Here are some examples of values:
- Personal Values: Honesty, integrity, independence, kindness, compassion, creativity, adventure, learning, etc.
- Relationship Values: Communication, respect, trust, support, shared interests, emotional intimacy, etc.
- Life Values: Purpose, contribution, growth, joy, balance, etc.

Step 2: Jot down those core values and beliefs.

Step 3: Pick out moments where your actions might have been influenced by others. Are you doing things just to please someone else? Write those down.

Step 4: Now, look at your list. Does it describe who you truly are, or do you see some things that are more about pleasing others than staying true to yourself?

Step 5: Put your values on a ranking scale. Give each value a ranking based on its importance to you. This helps you understand what matters most and where you may need to make adjustments.

Step 6: Start integrating your values into your daily life. Before you make any decision or take action, check to see if they align with the values you hold dear.

Step 7: It's not always easy, but try sticking to your values even when faced with challenges. This will help build a stronger connection with your true self.

Step 8: Set a reminder to revisit your values and beliefs occasionally. Your priorities may have taken a different form. The older and wiser you get, the more your priorities change.

Step 9: Talk to a close friend about your values and beliefs. They can offer insights and maybe even help you stay on track when things get confusing.

Step 10: Acknowledge and celebrate when you make decisions that align with the new things you've discovered about yourself. Pat yourself on the back for staying true to what matters most to you.

The Challenges of Self-Discovery

Geraldine and Marcus seem like the perfect couple. They love each other so much they can't bear to be away from each other. They met during a rough time in both of their lives, and they latched on to each other, finding solace in each other's company. That is the perfect breeding ground for a codependent relationship dynamic. What began as occasional support morphed into a constant duet, with each note of joy, sadness, or anger needing the other's presence in order to feel complete. They became each other's emotional crutches, leaning heavily on the other's validation to feel secure and understood. However, as time passed, Geraldine began to feel bad about the amount of time she spent with her boyfriend. The older she got, the more she realized that she had no identity of her own.

Facing the Uncomfortable Truth

The more Geraldine pondered about her new feelings, the more she realized she had to confront the uncomfortable truth about the nature of her relationship. The young woman made time for herself to really think about her life and realized that she had indeed been shutting down all of her aspirations and dreams just to be with Marcus. She was always neglecting her own needs for the sake of maintaining peace and love in their relationship. She wanted to confront Marcus about it, but she was filled with anxiety and fear every time she considered talking to him about it.

A Change Is Near

The simple idea of a change strikes two very distinct chords in the young woman. Geraldine is excited and terrified at the same time about breaking free from the codependent relationship. She really wanted to move on to clear the grass on her path and become her own person. She was constantly worried about losing her lover's comfort and familiar arms. Even now, she has realized that this relationship is holding her back, yet she can't bring herself to leave because Marcus has become her "comfort zone." How does she break out, then?

Strategies to Navigate Challenges with Resilience and Self-Compassion

Self-Reflection: Geraldine had to first self-reflect. She took time to filter through her thoughts and emotions to find clarity. She needed to face the truth about how her actual needs and desires were not being met because of the relationship she was in. Taking time to self-reflect gave Geraldine the room to confront their situation's ugliness and uncomfortable truths.

Seeking Support: The young woman struggled for some time, then finally decided it would be much less scary if she told someone about it. So, she went out to seek support. Geraldine found someone to talk to in the company of her friends and family. She told them all about her struggles and listened as they gave her their valuable perspective, reassuring her that she wouldn't go through this time of change alone.

Drawing a Line: Geraldine learned that she needed to set healthy boundaries within her relationship with Marcus. She made sure she spoke up about her needs assertively and advocated for her own well-being. The boundary she succeeded in instilling helped her regain a bit of self-respect and a sense of autonomy.

Exploring New Interests: No longer willing to keep Marcus as the center of focus and attention, Geraldine decided to explore activities and hobbies that brought her joy and fulfillment. She now engages in new experiences that allow her to see what she is really passionate about. She rediscovered her interests and lost passions, which, when explored, rewarded her with a sense of self-confidence and independence.

Accepting Change: It took a while, but Geraldine had to embrace the changes that came with self-discovery. She pushed her fears aside, kept Marcus's face away from the line of sight of her mind's eye, and submerged herself into the waters of change for personal growth. She knew that change is very – correctly – constant in life. She approached it with an open mind, willing to learn and unlearn as she discovered who she really was.

Practicing Self-Compassion: Throughout her journey, Geraldine made it a point to show more love to herself. She was patient with her growth process, offering herself kindness and understanding in the moments when she felt like she had made the wrong choice for breaking out. Every time she had doubts or criticisms, she reminded herself that self-discovery was a gradual process and that it was okay to stumble sometimes along the way. She was determined to make it through. You can do the same.

Activity 3: A Reflective Journaling Session to Unmask Your Authentic Self

Imagine yourself literally taking off a mask that represents everything that is holding your authentic self back and hidden.

https://www.pexels.com/photo/woman-wearing-a-mardi-gras-mask-9391383/

Do you sometimes feel like you're wearing someone else's costume in real life? Like there's someone else inside of you, screaming and clawing at your insides to break free? This journaling session is your invitation to peel off those layers and connect with the hidden parts of your personality to experience fulfillment. Now, grab that favorite pen of yours and find a quiet place. It's time for an honest, insightful journey into the hidden parts of yourself. Follow these steps to get started and find the answers you're seeking.

Step 1: Close your eyes and take a deep breath. Think of a limitless horizon. Imagine it stretching before you. What do you see? What kind of adventures unfold in it? Write down the first three dreams that come to mind, no matter how big or "impossible" they might seem.

Ask Yourself These Questions:
- What really gets me pumped and excited?
- Are there dreams I've buried because of fear or lack of confidence?
- What can I do to change the situation and bring my dreams back to life?

Step 2: If you were standing at the edge of a dark alley, you would wonder what species of beings lurk within the shadows? Is it safe to enter? A huge part of you (the part that wants to remain alive) will scream at you to turn back and run away. Your codependent relationship will make everyone and everything else look like a dark alley. Write down three things that scare you the most, be it failure, judgment, or vulnerability. Remember, there's no shame in acknowledging your fears.

Ask Yourself These Questions:
- What beliefs do I have that are holding me back from chasing after dreams earnestly?
- Where does this fear come from?
- Can I turn my fear into a motivating challenge?
- How can I build my courage and resilience to face these fears?

Step 3: Picture yourself in a masquerade ball. Now, slowly remove the mask you're wearing. Who are you under it? Describe three unexpected or hidden aspects of your personality you only allow to come and play when you're alone and away from the rest of the world.

Ask Yourself These Questions:
- Why am I scared of showing this part of myself?
- Will I be a different person if I let the hidden parts of myself come to light?
- How can I create a safe space to express my true self more freely?

Step 4: Re-read your entries. Reflect on them. Did you find any connection between your dreams, fears, and hidden self? Now, how do they influence your current choices and relationships? Take some time to reflect on this newfound information.

Ask Yourself These Questions:
- What is one action I can take today to live more as my true self, be comfortable in my skin, and be aligned with my dreams?
- How can I push back at my fears and overcome limiting beliefs to step into my full potential?
- Who can I contact for support on this journey of finding myself?

Activity 4: Crafting a Personal Mission Statement

It's time to translate those discoveries from the previous section into a powerful tool for personal growth: your personal mission statement.

Step 1: Pull out your journaling entries from the previous activity. Reread them with fresh eyes. Highlight phrases, words, or emotions that resonate deeply. Are there any recurring themes? What aspects of yourself are you most excited to embrace?

Ask Yourself These Questions:
- What values do I want to uphold throughout my life?
- What kind of impact do I want to make on the world?
- What qualities do I admire in others?
- How can I develop those admirable qualities myself?

Step 2: Write a letter to your future self, one filled with hope, purpose, and unwavering support. What message would you give them? If a letter is too old school for you, then write yourself a personal mission statement. Think of it as a letter to the future you condensed into a powerful declaration. Start with phrases like "I will..." or "I am dedicated to..." and add your values, aspirations, and unique strengths.

Ask Yourself These Questions:

- How can I combine my dreams with my values to create a fulfilling purpose?
- How can I phrase my statement to be clear, inspiring, and meaningful?

Step 3: Your mission statement isn't set in stone. You can refine it from time to time. It's a living document that changes alongside you. Don't be afraid to revise and refine it as you grow and discover more about yourself. Revisit it regularly, perhaps during birthdays or moments of self-reflection. Use it as a compass to guide your choices and remind you of who you are meant to be.

Ask Yourself These Questions:

- Does my mission statement still resonate with me after some time has passed?
- Are there new experiences or discoveries that need to be added to it?
- How can I use my mission statement to make decisions that keep me on the right path of exploring my true self?

The Liberating and Empowering Experience of Self-discovery

If you ever need reasons to break out of a codependent relationship and find yourself, take a look at these:

1. After confronting your fears and limiting thoughts, you emerge with newfound courage. You can now set healthy boundaries and say "no" to people's faces without any guilt. Isn't that liberating to think about?
2. When you stand your ground, you begin to attract people who appreciate your true self. This will enable you to create even deeper connections. People are more likely to open up about themselves when they perceive you as authentic.
3. What about your potential? That takes off, too. As you reconnect with your dreams and values, your passion comes alive again, and you are driven to pursue your unique destiny.

The sky becomes your starting point.
4. By the time you're radiating with self-worth and self-confidence, you'll become a beacon of inspiration to others going through your past experiences. You have now tasted the power of self-discovery.

Section 7: From Codependency to Interdependence

Imagine thinking of a person, and the first thing that comes to mind is that you can't picture life without them or that you would do everything for them, regardless of how this may affect you. That is how people in codependent relationships feel. In contrast, people in interdependent relationships, while grateful for others" presence in their lives, know that they would thrive alone as well. Their relationship is built on boundaries and mutual respect. At the same time, each person maintains their independence, enabling them to thrive as individuals.

The goal is to go from codependence to interdependence, where you have healthy individual lives together.

https://www.pexels.com/photo/happy-young-multiracial-couple-taking-on-sofa-at-home-1049517/

The goal of breaking from a codependent relationship is to reach interdependence. Showcasing the transition from unhealthy relationship dynamics to a balanced, supportive bond, this chapter will teach you how to steer away from the enmeshment characterized by codependency.

The Traits of Interdependent Relationships

In short, interdependence is a state of relationships where both parties can be independent but also support each other in a healthy way. Still, as relationships can be vastly different, so can the traits of interdependence occurring in them. Below are some of the core characteristics of these mutually supportive and fulfilling relationships.

Boundaries

In interdependent relationships, there are always clear boundaries. All parties know what they can expect from each other and what the others will or will not tolerate. This is a stark contrast to codependent relationships, where the lines are blurred, leading people to disrespect them (even without being aware of it) and many hurt feelings.

Say a coworker asks you to cover for them because they can't complete their work for the third time in a month. You already have a lot on your plate, and you know that picking up after your colleague will make it even harder to finish your obligations. Plus, this isn't the first time they've asked you for this. You say no, clearly stating that you can't help them because your schedule is full, and suggest that they should try to work on their schedule to ensure they won't be late on their assignments all the time.

Autonomy

Interdependent relationships are like a sports team. Everyone puts in their independent strengths and supports each other in overcoming each other's weaknesses. No one has to give up their autonomy just because they're on the team and have to support their teammates. Everyone can work on themselves, striving toward fulfilling their passions and goals. Moreover, they feel confident that they can do this even if the other person(s) on the team isn't there to support them.

For example, in an interdependent romantic relationship, both partners support each other's passions, giving each other ample time and opportunities to grow. They can spend quality time with their families and friends separately – without the other person feeling left out. They know that spending time apart is much better for their relationships because it allows both of them to find fulfillment, making them happier.

Clear Communication Lines

Communication is key in every relationship, but the quality of this communication is important. Those in interdependent relationships can always convey their needs and wants clearly and effectively. They can be honest with each other, leaving no room for misunderstanding or hurt feelings.

People's interdependent relationships can't reach other's minds, so they know that to maintain a healthy relationship, they must take the initiative to talk about whatever is on their minds. If miscommunication occurs, they will have a calm and rational conversation about the issue without letting their hurt feelings make them resort to conflicts.

Communication is particularly fundamental when it comes to making monumental decisions in any area of life. For example, suppose two business partners have different ideas on how to spruce up their brand. In that case, each can outline their list of reasons why they think their idea could work better. Then, they can sit down and review each other's lists, discussing each point to reach a resolution.

Compromise

Interdependent relationships are about give and take. Both parties get equal attention and respect for their wants and needs. While they both understand they must make big decisions together, they can respect it if one person makes a small decision because it supports their needs. The other person will support this decision because they know they will get the same consideration when they make a similar choice to support their happiness.

At no point will one person become the sole center of attention. Sometimes, people have different views on life. However, even if the other person doesn't fully agree with the decision that has been made, they can understand that respecting it benefits their entire relationship, so they're willing to compromise. The key is that all parties have to put aside their own views at times, and it isn't only one person doing this, as it happens in codependent relationships.

Compromise can be big or small. For example, two roommates can agree that they'll split the living costs each month. For one month, one roommate pays for rent, and the other pays the bill for utilities and groceries. Next month, it will be the other way around.

An example of a bigger compromise would be establishing boundaries. Each party gives up something when they agree to respect the other person's lines, but they also gain benefits from the relationship.

Mutual Respect

Healthy relationships are built on mutual respect. All parties acknowledge that they may have differences of opinion and are willing to provide due consideration to the other person's views. They can listen to each other openly and without judgment and criticism, which allows them to understand where everyone is coming from.

Interdependence also enables people to respect other people's boundaries. For example, if in a romantic relationship, one partner says that they're uncomfortable with public displays of affection, the other partner will respect this.

In interdependent relationships, everyone respects each other's goals and dreams. Even if one person aspires to something different from the other, they'll get the support they need and won't have to worry about being looked down on for having their individual desires.

Safety and Security

Interdependent relationships are a safe space where everyone feels secure and reassured that they can be vulnerable and honest when expressing their thoughts and emotions. They know they won't be judged, criticized, or discouraged from conveying what's on their mind and heart.

At the same time, interdependence also allows people to give honest feedback without the other person getting offended or step back without interfering with the other person's decision, even if they disagree.

Suppose one partner in a romantic relationship says they need a little more space. In that case, the other person won't get upset and start an argument. They'll express genuine concern and reassure their partner that they are there for them if they are ready to talk about their reasons. They'll ask if there is anything they can do to support the partner but wait until they're ready to talk about the issue.

Accountability

Arguments and conflicts happen in all relationships. The question is whether a person will own up to the actions that led to the disagreement. In codependent dynamics, one person often takes the easy way out by blaming the other person for everything that goes wrong in their relationship. Interdependence, on the other hand, is about recognizing one's own mistakes and taking responsibility for them.

Everyone makes mistakes, and no one is perfect. There is nothing wrong with admitting you did something wrong or need help. If a parent is upset with an adult child for neglecting to finish a chore, the child should admit they were wrong and not make an excuse. They may be distracted, and they can acknowledge their fault, saying they'll do it as soon as possible. If they're struggling with something, they can explain that they have a lot on their plate and need help.

Are Your Relationships Codependent or Interdependent?

If you aren't sure whether your current relationships lean toward interdependence or codependence, the following quiz will help you. It enables you to access your connection against the criteria of interdependence, helping you identify areas that need improvement.

Choose the statement that best describes each of your relationships.

Thinking about your romantic partner, what would you say?
- My partner completes me, and I can't live my life without them.
- My partner and I make a great team, and I am happy they're part of my life.

You're invited to a friend's birthday party without your partner. Do you feel the following?
- You need to ask your partner's permission to go to the party.
- You can go ahead and make plans to attend the party and only inform your partner that you are going.

Your friend calls you to help them move. It's a last-minute call, and you have a busy schedule ahead of you. Do you:
- Drop all your plans and head to your friends to help them out because you feel they'll get upset if you don't.
- You tell them you're sorry but have a lot on your plate and can't accommodate them now.

Your friend calls you because they're having an issue with their partner and need someone to unburden themselves to. This isn't the first time, and you listened to them plenty of times, but when you need to talk to someone, they are always too busy to listen. What do you do?

- Ask them when you can meet up to talk because you feel sorry they're upset. They're your friend, and you feel that you always have to be there for them.
- Tell them you're sorry they're going through tough times, but you can't always be there for them.

You're planning to cut your hair to change up your look a little bit. When approaching your partner about this idea, you:

- Ask their opinion and make a decision based on what they say.
- Tell them your reasons for wanting to cut your hair, listen to their opinion, but decide on the haircut anyway because it's ultimately your choice.

Your relationships are codependent if you checked the first answers in each pairing. If you checked the second one, your dynamics are more likely to be interdependent.

How to Cultivate Interdependence

Converting codependence into interdependence is a challenging but not impossible feat. It will take some work because it will bring up uncomfortable truths and hidden fears. You may even worry whether your relationship can survive this shift or whether you'll lose the other person.

Negative aspects notwithstanding, taking a chance by bringing positive changes to make your relationship dynamics healthier is worth it. Your connection will be stronger and longer-lasting, and the two of you will be happier individually and together.

Transforming a codependent connection involves tackling each person's actions, thoughts, and feelings individually and within the relationship. The first step, opening up a dialogue about the change, is always the hardest. Yet, it's crucial to talk about the dependency issue. Here are a few tips to help you out:

Work on Yourself

In a healthy relationship, people respect each other's individual wants and needs, but this can't be the only way to feed your self-worth. You must work on your self-esteem separately from your relationship.

Most people value how others see them and try to live up to this picture, which is exactly the problem with codependency. Ask yourself, "Would I see myself differently if I wasn't receiving this feedback from another person." Would you be as confident without getting this validation? If not, it's time to work on your self-esteem.

By boosting your confidence, you'll be able to contribute to your relationship far more than if you just rely on the other person for some pick-me-up. When both people in the relationship are secure in their personal lives, insecurities and over-reliance become part of the past.

Enjoy Your Life Outside the Relationship

While spending time with your loved ones can be fun, enjoying time apart is also good. To build a healthy, interdependent relationship, make time to pursue what's important to you, even if these are interests you don't share with the other person.

Make a list of hobbies and interests you enjoyed before your relationship began. You can also find new goals to pursue. Whatever path you take, give yourself room to prioritize personal passions and encourage others to do the same.

Have Friends in Common but Also Separately

People's social circles evolve both within and separately from their relationships. You can bond with other people's loved ones but can also nurture and widen your own personal social circle.

Mutual connections will be a source of comfort and support for the relationship as a whole, whereas individual connections will give you distance and an opportunity to reach for advice without incurring conflicting interests.

Set Boundaries

Boundaries, especially the ones revolving around each person's time and energy, are the foundation of every healthy relationship. Setting emotional, physical, mental, and energy-related boundaries will protect your relationship.

Making it clear how much quality time you need, creating ways to start uncomfortable conversations, feeling safe to say no, and much more are boundaries that bring many benefits to individual people in the relationship and the unit as a whole.

When the limits are set, all parties should understand and accept them without feeling rejected or attacked personally. The best way to approach this is to view the other person's boundary from their perspective. Thinking about what it gives them will allow you to respect the lines they are drawn.

Negotiate Mutually Agreeable Outcomes

Think of every conversation about difficult or sensitive topics and disagreements as a team-building exercise. In a team, members must rely on each other to complete the tasks and support each other to reach a better outcome.

When having these talks, sit down with the conscious intention of negotiating a solution that's fulfilling for both parties. This will teach you selflessness, compassion, and honesty. Those are all the qualities you need to understand the benefits of investing in each other's happiness.

Support Each Other's Personal Growth

While every person can thrive independently in a relationship, they don't have to do everything alone. The key is to find the balance between respecting each other's boundaries and supporting each other's personal growth.

How this support looks depends on the individual relationship dynamics. It may be as simple as being there for the other person during a big milestone they reach while pursuing their interests.

Don't Be Afraid to Be Vulnerable

Sometimes, you'll be reluctant to bring up a discussion because you know it could make you look vulnerable or simply because you want to avoid conflict. However, in healthy relationships, the parties have space to be vulnerable, encouraging them to lead every dialogue with empathy instead of anger.

Working toward interdependence means learning to accept that no one is perfect. It's much easier to acknowledge one's faults and mistakes, knowing that the other person has them too, and they won't judge or criticize.

At the same time, showing vulnerability takes the kind of courage only confident people are capable of displaying, bringing the process to the full circle. By working on your self-esteem, you're empowering yourself to overcome fears that may be affecting your relationships.

Relationship Growth Plan

The best way to move from codependency to healthier relationship dynamics is to set goals and outline steps to foster interdependence in your relationships. Devising a relationship growth plan can help you with this task.

Consider the following steps to grow your relationship. Discussing each one openly with the other person is crucial, as well as defining why you want to take each step and how it may benefit the relationship.

Step 1: Agree to Disagree

Make peace with the fact that you won't always be right, and neither will the other person in the relationship. Make the conscious choice that when one of you disagrees with the other person's opinion or actions, you will simply let it go without resentment. This simple act of letting go will help you in a relationship and give you a newfound sense of contentment.

Step 2: Check on Each Other's Interests Regularly

Just because two people in a relationship have different fulfilling hobbies, it doesn't mean they can't share them with each other. Taking the effort to step into the world the other person enjoys shows that you are genuinely interested in what makes them happy. Create a list of things both of you enjoy and set a reminder to ask the other person about these regularly.

_____

_____

_____

_____

_____

_____

Step 3. Talk Regularly

Regular dialogues with the other person will allow you to express your thoughts and feelings about your relationship dynamics, show them love and support whenever necessary, and bring the two of you much closer.

Step 4. Have Fun

Nothing can bring two people closer together than having a good time. Life is filled with challenges, and relationships are often punctuated with conflicts, but neither should stop you from having fun together. Schedule a time when the two of you can spend quality time doing something you both enjoy.

Step 5. Be Grateful

One of the key tenets of interdependent relationships is not taking the other person's presence for granted. Expressing your gratitude will help you grow your connection. Make it a habit to share what you're grateful for with each other while spending time together. This mutual exchange of appreciation will help you see how much you have, even when times are tough.

You can even create a list of what you're grateful for in the space below.

_____

_____

_____

_____

_____

_____

Step 6. Provide Positive Reinforcement

Providing positive feedback is one of the most impactful ways to bring your relationship to the next level. Both of you should pay attention when the other person does something good for you or your relationship and say "thank you." By showing you appreciate this act, each of you encourages the other person to continue the behavior.

Write down a few encouraging words you would like to hear from each other.

_____

_____

_____

_____

_____

_____

Step 7. Go the Extra Mile

While your relationship should be built on mutual support, at times, one of you will need more help than the other. It's crucial to be there when the other person needs you the most, even if it means giving up on something on your part. The best thing about this is that in healthy, interdependent relationships, you can expect the same when the tables turn.

Step 8. Give Each Other Space

Respect each other's independence. Whether pursuing a hobby or spending quality time with family and friends outside your relationships, the freedom to be yourself will help you create a stronger bond.

Create two lists, one for one person's interests and the other for the other person's interests. Then, discuss how much time you would like to spend on each.

_____

_____

_____

_____

_____

Interdependent relationships are all about bringing fulfillment into people's lives. They enrich the dynamics by allowing all parties to thrive both independently and together. Based on mutual respect and boundaries, interdependence is the ultimate key to healthy relationships.

As you move away from codependency and work toward living independently in an interdependent relationship, you'll experience plenty of positive changes. You will feel liberated and free to express your wants and needs, supported and respected by the other person, and won't be plagued by worries of being judged for your opinions and actions.

Even if you make mistakes, you'll know that the other person will understand because they aren't perfect either and will own up to their actions as well. All these positive changes will make your confidence soar.

Section 8: Communicating to Improve Interactions with Others

"Communication is key" is one of those phrases you're bound to hear at some point in your life. Whether with friends, family, or co-workers, you need to learn how to get your point across to avoid conflicts and misunderstandings. Communication can make or break a relationship. Sometimes, when you have a problem with someone, all you need to do is sit with them and talk. Learning to have healthy conversations can transform your relationships and move you away from the negative patterns of codependency.

This chapter provides effective communication strategies and activities to improve your personal and professional relationships.

Developing communication skills and strategies goes a long way in fostering healthy relationships.
https://www.pexels.com/photo/happy-couple-looking-at-each-other-6270008/

The Power of Effective Communication

Many of your relationship problems can be solved with good communication. When two people communicate their needs, they can reach a mutual understanding instead of going back to the same problem over and over without any resolution.

Effective communication is the foundation of any healthy relationship. It enables you to convey your emotions and thoughts with empathy and clarity. It minimizes confusion, encourages teamwork, resolves disputes, and creates close relationships.

Learning Each Other's Needs

Codependent individuals can be people pleasers, so they always neglect their own needs to keep their partners happy. Their inability to handle criticism can also be a problem for their loved ones, who may keep their feelings bottled up inside to avoid hurting them.

Effective communication can create a safe space for each of you to communicate your needs and know each other better. You can't support your loved ones or be there for them until you understand their hopes and dreams and what they expect from this relationship.

When was the last time you did something you love instead of always going along with what your friends want? Don't you wish you could connect with your loved ones just to know them better, without worrying about other intentions?

Get to know the people in your life, have deep conversations, ask questions, and be curious about them without being nosy.

Questions to Ask Your Loved Ones:

- How have you been feeling lately?
- What can I do to help you in your time of need?
- How is your job going these days?
- Is there anything you want me to do more or less?

Always ask straightforward questions. Take turns with your partner and let them also get to know you.

Resolving Conflicts

Lack of communication is almost always the reason behind conflicts in relationships. It leads to misunderstanding and constant fighting. During a conflict, codependent people may also refrain from being entirely honest because of their fear of abandonment, and they will just say what the other person wants to hear. The issue will remain unresolved.

Communication helps you resolve arguments faster as it allows each person to explain their side. When there's a problem, people usually start arguing and end up saying things they later regret. Healthy communication allows you to identify your feelings so you can calmly address them. For instance, your friend was supposed to help you paint your child's room but canceled at the last minute without any explanation. You see them a couple of days later at the gym, and they act as if nothing happened. Naturally, you are mad at them and want to express your anger.

You have two options: yell at them and call them rude or disrespectful, or tell them how their behavior hurt your feelings. When you get aggressive, the other person will get defensive, and a simple argument can escalate. However, when you calmly communicate with them, they will have an insight into your emotions and will respond accordingly.

Imagine these two scenarios:

Scenario A: Your friend yelling, "I am mad at you. What you did was horrible and insensitive."

Scenario B: Your friend says, "I am hurt and upset. You are my best friend, and I wasn't expecting this from you."

How would you react in both situations? In the first one, your friend isn't trying to communicate with you or make space for a healthy conversation. They are yelling, attacking, and accusing you. Naturally, you will get defensive and respond angrily.

In the second scenario, your friend is communicating their feelings. They aren't raising their voice or trying to fight. Also, their use of words shows they are hurting, which gives you the chance to show empathy. You will respond calmly by either apologizing or explaining yourself. You will end up resolving the conflict and putting it behind you.

Codependent people need to understand the power of effective communication during conflicts. Intense situations can drive you to dysfunctional patterns. Learning healthy communication strategies will prevent arguments from turning into fights and destroying your relationships.

Building Trust

Trust is often an issue with people suffering from fear of abandonment. Although this is related to childhood trauma, healthy communication can build trust. For instance, instead of accusing your partner of cheating or pushing them away, you can tell them about your fears and insecurities. You can tear down your walls and let them in, allowing them to see the weak and vulnerable parts you keep hidden from the world. Explain to them why you have trust issues.

The people in your life need to understand the reason behind your actions so they can adjust their behavior and response. Your partner will be more honest and open with you, so you will feel safer in the relationship.

Increasing Your Bond

People connect and bond with each other through communication. Long phone calls and deep conversations turn friends into best friends and strangers into lovers. You get to talk about your feelings, experiences, thoughts, and common interests.

People with a fear of abandonment often focus on the negative side of their relationships. This makes it easier to believe that everyone will eventually leave.

Communication goes beyond knowing the other person. You also share an emotional connection. When you communicate and learn about their strengths and weaknesses, you will see they also have fears and a vulnerable side. Maybe you will find that they are also afraid of abandonment or experienced childhood trauma. You will stop seeing them as someone who might hurt you and start seeing them as a wounded person looking for love and acceptance.

Setting Boundaries

Codependent people struggle with setting boundaries. You may not know how to say "No" or explain what behavior you don't tolerate. Effective communication skills enable you to speak up if you feel uncomfortable. You will be able to communicate your boundaries to avoid any misunderstandings in the future.

Signs of Poor Communication in a Relationship

- Overreacting to normal situations
- Only communicating via text messages or emails
- Always bringing up past mistakes during an argument

- Always blaming each other
- You keep having the same arguments
- Not actively listening to one another
- Defensive behavior during arguments
- Lack of trust
- Passive-aggressive behavior
- Lack of emotional intimacy
- Constant interruption during conversations
- Giving each other the silent treatment
- Harboring resentment
- Competitiveness
- Aggression
- Constant misunderstandings

Activity

Reflect on all your past relationships and your communication patterns. Identify all your poor communication behaviors like passive aggression or overreactions.

_____

_____

_____

_____

_____

Components of Healthy Communication

Healthy communication goes beyond expressing yourself. You should also actively listen to the other person, read their body language, and much more.

Active Listening

When was the last time you actually listened to someone? Nowadays, everyone seems distracted. They are either texting or checking social media when someone is talking to them, while others are only waiting for you to finish so they can start talking. Healthy communication requires you to actively listen to the people in your life.

Active listening involves more than hearing what the other person is saying. You are processing, understanding, and analyzing the meaning behind every word. You are trying to figure out the emotions they are conveying. This skill requires you to be completely focused and mindful during the conversation.

Active listening means listening to understand the other person's point of view from their perspective.
https://www.pexels.com/photo/elderly-man-looking-romantically-at-his-wife-8139241/

Active listening can improve your relationships by making the other person feel heard and understood. You learn that when someone is talking, it is more about them than you. For instance, your best friend has broken up with their partner. They are crying and telling you how they are feeling. You shouldn't interrupt them to tell them what you are thinking but should wait for them to finish to give them your opinion. They need empathy and understanding. Just be a shoulder for them to cry on. All they want is to be heard.

Tips for Active Listening
- Be fully present by ignoring distractions, avoiding daydreaming, and putting away your cell phone.
- Pay attention to their body language, facial expression, and tone of voice.
- Maintain eye contact.
- Avoid "Yes" or "No" questions and ask open-ended ones instead to keep the conversation flowing, like "What do you think?" or "Can you tell me more about it?"
- Reflect on what the person has said to make them feel validated, like "In other words, you are considering quitting your job" or "I hear that you are very upset."
- Ask for clarification if you don't understand what they are saying.
- Be patient, and don't interrupt them. Don't jump in and finish their sentences.
- Give them time to finish their thoughts.
- Listen to understand, not respond.
- Don't change the subject until they finish what they want to say.
- Don't judge.

Conversation Example:

Jack: I know you are busy, but I need to talk to someone. I had a huge fight with my wife.

Colin: Oh, sorry to hear that. What happened?

Jack: She got mad when I told her I had to go to China for work for a month. I can't believe her.

Colin: That's awful. You sound frustrated.

Jack: I am. It is just a month, and I am going to call her every day. So, what's her problem?

Colin: This is bad. How are you feeling about all of that?

Jack: I am mad, but I also feel guilty because I am going to leave her with the baby for a month.

Colin: This is a complicated situation. It looks like you need more time to work things out.

Jack: You are right. Thank you for listening. I needed that.

Assertiveness

Assertive communication is being direct and clear without dismissing the other person's feelings or disrespecting them. This prevents conflicts and misunderstandings and improves your relationships. It also helps you set boundaries as you learn to be assertive about your limits and say no when you feel uncomfortable.

Codependent people and people with a fear of abandonment need to use this skill. It encourages them to confidently express their needs and stand up for themselves when someone crosses their boundaries.

Assertiveness is different from aggression. Aggression involves crossing boundaries, disrespecting others, and forcing your needs on them. Assertiveness is about respecting other people's boundaries and communicating your needs.

It reduces anxiety, creates trust, reduces stress, encourages positive relationships, and boosts your self-esteem.

Tips for Assertive Communication:
- Maintain eye contact
- Acknowledge other people's feelings
- Use positive language
- Avoid blame or threats
- Use clear words to convey your message
- Avoid manipulation
- Be open and honest
- Stand or sit in a confident posture
- Avoid judgments
- Don't exaggerate. Instead of saying, "You are late, and you have ruined the whole day." Say, "We now don't have time to go to the movies, so we will just head to the restaurant."

Avoid "You" Statements

Statements starting with "You" can appear accusatory or judgmental. The other person will, in turn, become defensive, and you will end up fighting instead of solving the issue. Don't solely focus on what they did but on how their actions affected you.

Use "I" statements since they don't convey blame or trigger a defensive reaction.

Consider these two examples:
- "You need to stop interrupting me when I am speaking."
- "I would like it if you don't interrupt me when I am speaking."

The first statement feels like an attack, while in the second one, you are simply expressing your feelings.

Focus on Your Feelings

When you want to discuss someone's actions or behavior, you should also include how it made you feel. This allows for direct communication without making the other person feel judged or attacked. Like the previous point, you express how their behavior has affected you. You can say, "When you don't call me all day, I feel ignored and unappreciated."

Empathy

Empathy is the ability to put yourself in another person's shoes to understand their feelings and thoughts. Use this skill when you are actively listening to understand the other person's motivations and emotions. Empathetic people can create deep bonds and connections with the people in their lives. You will also be able to respond properly, validate other people's feelings, and accept them without judgment.

This skill will come in handy when you are delivering news to someone. You will be able to see things from their perspective and guess how they will react to the news.

Clarity

Make sure your message is clear and to the point. Don't beat around the bushes or use long introductions. Before you speak, take a moment to arrange your thoughts and figure out what you want to communicate so your words are understood and organized. Be straightforward and use simple language.

Don't give hints or ask questions. For instance, don't say, "I can't remember the last time we went out for dinner." Or "Do you want to go out for dinner?" Instead, say, "I'd like us to go out for dinner tonight." Your statements should be clear and express your feelings, thoughts, and needs.

Avoid ramblings, as they can create misunderstandings.

Non-Verbal Communication

Non-verbal communication is your body language, facial expressions, and tone of voice. Most people only listen to what you are saying and ignore the rest because they think your words are more significant. Interestingly, 80% of communication is non-verbal. It is also the most honest part of a conversation. People may lie, but it is very hard to fake your body language.

During a conversation, a person may not reveal everything to you, but you can guess what they are hiding by observing their body language. For instance, your best friend's ex got engaged. They smile and say they are happy for them. When you pay close attention, you can see that their lips are smiling, but their eyes aren't, meaning their smile isn't genuine. Or you can hear from their tone of voice that they are about to cry.

Learning non-verbal communication enables you to understand what someone is trying to communicate to you even when they aren't speaking so you can be there for them.

Non-verbal communication strengthens relationships, adds clarity to the conversation, and makes the person feel seen and understood.

Don't make assumptions if you feel someone is acting differently based on their body language. For instance, you may think that your coworker is upset when they are exhausted. So always ask them what's wrong. You can say, "You have been frowning all day. Are you okay?

Noticing non-verbal cues can be tricky because each person's body language is different. However, it is easier to read those close to you. For instance, you know how your partner's face looks when they are angry and your best friend's body language when they are hiding something. The more you observe people, the easier it will be to read these cues.

Communication Barriers

Communication barriers in codependent relationships can make social interactions difficult. There are a few strategies, however, that you can use to overcome these barriers.

Fear of Conflict

Many codependent individuals are people-pleasers. They will try to avoid conflict by all means. They ignore their feelings and needs and do as their partner says. Even if the other person is abusive or controlling, they will still agree with them on everything. They fear their loved ones will abandon them if they disagree or have a different opinion.

Fear of conflict prevents them from communicating their needs and speaking up for themselves. They stay in bad relationships, feeling miserable and incomplete.

Overcoming Fear of Conflict

Before confronting someone, take a few moments to visualize the outcome. It will boost your confidence and prepare you for a difficult conversation.

Instructions:

1. Find a quiet room with no distractions.
2. Lie down or sit in a comfortable position and close your eyes.
3. Visualize yourself standing before the person you want to confront.
4. You are calm and confident and able to communicate your needs to them.
5. Imagine you both resolving the issue and being happy with the outcome.

Difficulty Expressing Your Needs

Codependent people struggle with expressing their needs. They don't set boundaries and lead a miserable life, living someone else's life. They exist only to make other people happy.

Tips to Express Your Needs

Learning to express your needs takes time. However, keep practicing until this skill comes naturally to you.

Identify Your Needs

You can't communicate your needs without actually knowing what they are at first. You probably have different expectations from each person in your life. Write down what you want from the people in your life at moments when you feel you need to say something.

Remain Calm

You may feel angry or resentful because your needs have been ignored for so long. As a result, the conversation can be heated or emotional. This will affect your communication, and you won't be able to understand each other at first. Have this conversation when you are both calm and ready for a serious and complex discussion.

Avoid Accusations

You may want to blame them for ignoring your needs all this time. However, this will only make them defensive, so remain calm.

Explain How They Can Support You

After communicating your needs, explain practical ways they can support you. For instance, you tell your friend that you feel frustrated because they are always late and wish they would be on time. You can suggest that they text or call you if they are running late so you can adjust your schedule.

Making Assumptions Rather Than Asking

One of the biggest barriers in communication is when people assume things about you and act on them instead of asking. For instance, your friend is having her wedding in Paris. She knows you don't like to fly, so she assumes you won't attend and doesn't invite you. You get upset when you find out she invited everyone but you. You don't like flying, but you still do it when you have to, and you would happily have flown for her. This would have been avoided if she had just asked.

Everyone is guilty of making assumptions. However, you can easily overcome this tendency.

Overcoming Making Assumptions

- If someone doesn't seem like themselves, don't assume that they may be angry or upset. Ask them, "Are you okay?" or "Is everything okay?"
- Don't make assumptions during a conversation; ask for clarification. "I am not sure what you mean. Can you elaborate?"
- If there is a misunderstanding, ask, "I am not sure what happened; can we talk about it?"
- When you use words like "I think they meant" or "I think they want," you are making assumptions. Stop yourself and just ask the person.

Activity

Start a "Communication Challenge" where you apply the techniques you learned here, like active listening or empathy, in your daily interactions. Record your experience and what you learned in your journal.

No one is born with communication skills. You learn it through practice and experience. Practice these techniques every day, and if you are struggling, try them on close family members or friends first. Similar to any skill, in time, you will master it. Self-reflect to assess your progress. Write down the areas that require improvement and work on them.

These skills will improve your relationships as they encourage you to be more honest and open so you will avoid conflict and misunderstandings. They also push you to speak up for yourself, communicate your needs, and be direct and honest, boosting your self-esteem and allowing for personal growth.

Section 9: Surviving and Thriving: Healing the Past and Maintaining Healthy Relationships

In this chapter, you'll understand how your past experiences affect your current and future relationships. You'll understand the link between your traumas and your codependent tendencies and learn about the steps you need to take to embark on your healing journey. You'll find activities that will help you acknowledge, process, and address your negative thoughts and feelings and let go of harmful experiences. This chapter also explores what a healthy relationship should look like and offers activities that will allow you to reflect on your current relationships and set tangible goals for your future ones.

Healing from the past will strengthen your relationships in the future.
https://www.pexels.com/photo/silhouette-of-woman-on-swing-during-golden-hour-289998/

How the Past Affects Your Current and Future Relationships

Have you ever noticed that you act a certain way in all your relationships? You have a fixed response to certain actions from your partners, have the same expectations from them, and feel the need to hide the same traits within yourself. While the thoughts, feelings, and behaviors that arise in a relationship largely depend on the relationship dynamics and each partner's unique traits, some aspects within yourself remain relatively the same. This is because how you act in your current relationship is a product of all that you've learned in the past. In a sense, your past relationships serve as a blueprint for your future ones.

Your past relationships are all you've ever known about being with a partner. You might have witnessed relationships through family members, friends, books, and movies throughout your life, but yours are the only practical experiences you've had. They influenced your perception of how love should look like.

Your non-romantic relationships, especially the ones you experience early in your life, also impact your non-romantic and romantic relationships. These interactions give you insight into what you should do and say when dealing with others. They help you define what a healthy relationship looks like based on your experiences. All your relationships influence your decisions regarding choosing a partner and interacting with them.

Negative past experiences can keep you stuck in your unhealthy ways. Many people who have experienced unhealthy relationships can struggle to maintain healthy current and future relationships, even when their partners are not to blame. They could constantly worry that all the relationships they'll form will mirror the past harmful ones, and so they are likely to start to become defensive, which often causes more harm than good.

Here are a few ways in which your past relationships can impact your current and future ones:

The Need to Replace a Lost Aspect of the Self

According to research that explored the impact of past relationships on future ones with the role of the self as a mediating variable, people who believe that their partners are a representation of their self-concept usually seek out new partners that resemble their past ones in terms of personality, hobbies, or physical traits. When your relationships are a factor that contributes to your overall sense of self, you subconsciously keep on choosing relationships with patterns and dynamics like your past ones. This even applies to factors like how long the relationships last or the time between breakups. The study reveals that this might be a way for people to replace the lost aspect of themselves following a breakup.

The Fear of Repeating the Past

One of the most common ways in which negative past experiences can impact future ones is through the fear of repeating what happened before. Those who have gone through traumatic or harmful experiences might feel anxious about building new relationships. They'll struggle to trust their new partner entirely, which would create problems. If your ex-partner cheated on you before, for instance, you may not be able to trust your new partner entirely. Even if they don't resemble your other partner in any way, you'll still feel on edge and anticipate their betrayal.

Having trust issues can cause you to need a lot of reassurance from your partner. You might also frantically ask them about their whereabouts or what they're doing on their phone. This behavior might frustrate your partner and put a strain on your relationship. Your fears are valid and aren't easy to let go of. The process requires a lot of external assistance. Regardless of where you are in your healing journey, you must be honest with your partner and transparent about your past experiences. Sharing what you went through can make them significantly more understanding and help them grasp the rationale behind your fears.

Comparing Your Relationships with Old Ones

Many people fall into the trap of comparing their old partners with their new ones. This, however, does more harm than good. It can be tempting to think about what your new partner does better or worse than your ex. You may also have great memories you want to relive or negative experiences you wish you never have to live through again. Regardless of why you're comparing your relationships, holding onto the past will prevent you from fully appreciating your partner and the experiences you get to have with them. It stops you from giving your current or future partners a fair chance. You'll never be with someone who is exactly the same as someone else. Each relationship has its unique downturns and upsides.

When reflecting on your old relationships, you must always keep in mind that the human brain is a trickster. It makes it seem like your memories were a lot better than they actually were, meaning that you may remember your past relationships in a better light. According to News Medical, the human brain may also block certain memories and leave out negative aspects of certain situations in cases of severe trauma.

Missing Out on the Present Moment

Spending a lot of time stuck in the past also keeps you from noticing what's going on in the present. Your mind is so obsessed with the memories and fears of your past experiences that you're unable to notice how special your current relationships are. Living in your memories keeps you from making new ones and forming new connections with friends, family, and romantic partners. It can be very difficult to move on from difficult incidents or experiences. By working with a professional, you can learn to be more present in the moment and live a happier life.

The Link between Traumas and Codependency

Living with trauma can be destructive to one's mental, emotional, and social health. Unresolved trauma can affect your relationships and lead to codependency. The only way to break the habit of codependency is to work through the underlying issues. Trauma manifests in various forms, all of which leave lasting consequences. Even if you consider yourself resilient, have a strong friends and family support network, or benefit from other protective factors, you can still experience the harrowing consequences of trauma. Trauma can lead to a wide range of mental conditions, such as stress, anxiety, depression, and PSTD, causing individuals to turn to unhealthy coping mechanisms, such as substance abuse, social withdrawal, or codependency, to alleviate their pain and establish a (false) sense of control.

Trauma is an emotional response to a difficult experience. Anyone can undergo or witness a traumatic incident; however, based on the severity of the event and other personal factors, some people are better at coping than others. Suppose you struggle to maintain healthy relationships or have other resulting mental or emotional conditions. In that case, you can benefit from seeking professional help to start the healing process and keep things from getting worse.

Most codependent relationships are a result of childhood trauma. This type of emotional response usually arises from familial issues, such as abuse, neglect, or witnessing violence and constant arguments. Familial relationships are the first social interactions a child forms in the world. When these interactions are unhealthy and harmful, the child grows up without witnessing what a healthy relationship should look like. The child might even start mimicking whatever they witness at home with their friends, and their actions or behaviors get mistaken for a child's tendency to misbehave.

While trauma can manifest as physical or verbal violence, it can often manifest as feelings of helplessness and excessive dependency. Adults who experienced childhood trauma may also try to offer their loved ones what they never received in life. They may care unduly for others and expect nothing in return. They feel their best when others depend on them, making the role of the caregiver their ultimate purpose in life.

Codependents who choose the wrong people to be friends or in a romantic relationship with don't realize they're in for another trap. While there are many good people in the world, others are likely to take advantage of a codependent individual's tendency to *over*care. Abusive individuals can use physical, emotional, or verbal violence to control their codependent partners. If you were ever in this situation, you may have felt ashamed for your inability to leave this relationship, even though it was clearly harmful to you.

This dynamic is known as trauma bonding and is a coping mechanism that often results from childhood trauma. It is characterized by the tendency to feel loyal to and dependent on your abuser. Abusers are great at what they do. They use a wide range of emotionally manipulative techniques, such as alternating between periods of affection and abuse, love-bombing, and gaslighting to make it difficult for their partners to recognize the abuse and break free. Trauma bonding can also occur in a codependent relationship without abuse, where the codependent individual is extremely attached to someone who isn't good for them. Breaking free from a trauma bond is usually the most difficult part. The healing process is long and hard but isn't as challenging.

The Healing Journey

The following are a few steps you can take to start healing from an unhealthy relationship and letting go of your codependent tendencies:

Acknowledge Your Feelings

Take the time to feel and understand your emotions. Sometimes, suppressing your feelings is the easiest choice. However, you'll stay stuck in the past if you don't face and address them. Allow yourself to process all the pent-up negative emotions you've accumulated through the years. Deal with your anger, grief, regret, frustration, and all feelings that arise so you can finally move on.

Prioritize Self-Care

To practice self-care, you must realize you're worthy of love, care, and compassion. You need to realize that your wants and needs are worth taking care of. Instead of building your entire life's purpose around your ability to care for others and cater to their comfort, work on redefining your perception of life. Why are happiness and self-fulfillment not your utmost purposes in life? Your personal goals and satisfaction should be your markers of success.

Your self-worth shouldn't be associated with your accomplishments, happiness, or other people's perceptions. Your worth goes beyond these trivial metrics. You're invaluable, and you deserve to be treated with respect. However, you can't expect others to treat you right if you can't do that yourself! Start honoring and respecting your thoughts, feelings, wants, and needs. Engage in hobbies and activities that you love and bring you comfort.

Practicing self-care and prioritizing your needs and wants is not selfish. Can you use your car to drive 4 miles if it only has enough fuel to drive you 2 miles? Just as you need to stop at a gas station to refuel your car, you need to recharge and prioritize yourself to interact with others and offer them healthy amounts of help and support. Prioritizing your wants and needs allows you to give time and effort to others within reasonable limits and ensures that you don't drain yourself in the process.

Reconnect with Friends and Family

When you're in a codependent relationship, you might get so caught up in your partner's needs that you don't pay enough time and effort to other people in your life. Codependent individuals don't realize they're gradually building a wall around their romantic relationship, which weakens their bonds with their friends and family. Now that you're trying to break free from this unhealthy habit, there's no better time to reach out to them to reconnect. Rebuilding these bridges can be the perfect way to gather the mental and emotional strength you need to let go of the past. Some friends and family members may be unwelcoming at first, especially if you've suddenly disappeared from their lives. However, they'll surely understand if you're transparent about your thoughts, feelings, and experiences.

Create and Maintain Boundaries

Setting and maintaining boundaries can be very difficult, especially if you've lived your whole life without them. When you value yourself and honor your wants and needs, it will be easier for you to say "no" to others and set healthy boundaries in your interactions. Take the time to think about what you expect from your family members, friends, and romantic partners in your relationships. Find out what you're willing to offer them – and learn to say "no" to things that you can't or don't want to do.

Regulate Your Emotional Responses

If you've been codependent for as long as you can remember, it can be very difficult to hear someone say that they're in trouble, feel down, or need help without feeling the overwhelming need to help. You're not responsible for fixing anyone's problems or finding solutions for them. Friends are there to help each other by offering emotional support. Sometimes, being a good listener and letting them know that you're there for them is enough.

Learn to Self-Soothe

You need to learn to self-soother to avoid resorting to unhealthy coping mechanisms whenever you feel overwhelmed by negative thoughts and feelings. Self-soothing involves doing anything that helps you feel safe and calm and brings you comfort. You could have a *comfort meal*, watch your favorite TV show, spend time with friends, listen to music, or go for a walk. Practicing meditation and mindfulness techniques can also be a great way to process and address these emotions and become more present in the moment.

Work With a Therapist

Letting go of the past and overcoming unhealthy coping mechanisms can be extremely challenging to do on your own. Consider working with a professional therapist who can help you understand your thoughts and feelings, process your past experiences, understand yourself more effectively, and figure out healthy ways to deal with overwhelming emotions. A therapist can also guide you toward honoring yourself, recognizing your value, and building and maintaining healthy boundaries with others.

Activity: Guided Imagery

This meditation will help you process, address, and soothe your past wounds.

1. Find a comfortable and quiet place. Make sure you won't be interrupted for the next few minutes. Practice deep breathing for the duration of this activity.
2. Close your eyes and visualize yourself in a setting that brings you peace, comfort, and happiness. If you imagine the beach, feel the breeze on your skin. If you're in a large, open field, imagine how the grass would feel on your bare feet. Try to

feel exactly how you would if you were there.
3. Notice a stream of flowing water. This stream symbolizes your thoughts, memories, and feelings. While still visualizing your place of comfort, think of a painful experience or memory that still affects you. Acknowledge all the thoughts and feelings that arise in this moment. Embrace them fully, no matter how hard it may be.
   1. After you've acknowledged your thoughts and feelings, create a paper boat in your mind and place the memory in it. Visualize yourself releasing the boat in the water, watching the memory float away and out of your sight.
   2. As you observe the boat while it floats away, imagine a warm light surrounding it. This light represents compassion and apprehension.
   3. Feel the sense of relief that washes over you now that you've let go of the negative thoughts and feelings that this memory brings.
   4. Return your attention to your breathing. Imagine that each deep inhale brings with it a sense of peace and renewal. Open your eyes and slowly bring your attention to the present moment.

Activity: A Letter to the Past

Write a letter to your past self, someone who has hurt you, or even a certain period or event in your life. Explore your thoughts and feelings and how this event or person impacts your life to this day. Reflect on what you've learned from this experience and how it has helped shape you into the person you are today. Use this letter as an opportunity to forgive yourself or the person who has hurt you, let go of the past, and acknowledge that you're ready to move on. You don't need to send this letter to anyone, as it's simply a way to express yourself and externalize your thoughts and emotions.

What a Healthy Relationship Looks Like

The following elements are key to building and maintaining healthy and lasting relationships:

Mutual Respect

Healthy boundaries are crucial to maintaining your mental, emotional, and physical health, as well as personal morals, values, and beliefs. Boundaries are also important for maintaining a level of respect between one another. Your boundaries communicate to others what is important to you and what they can do to make you feel safe, appreciated, and valued. Building a healthy relationship requires finding the right balance between intimacy and space. Both individuals should feel close – yet still make enough space for each other's thoughts and feelings.

Imagine you want to go out with your friends on the weekend, but your partner prefers to stay at home and relax. If you respect each other's feelings and desires, you will try to compromise and find common ground. For instance, you could agree to spend one weekend out with friends and another at home relaxing. This way, you would respect each other's social gatherings and relaxation needs.

Mutual Trust

Trust is the cornerstone of any relationship. You can't be friends or partners with someone you don't trust. You need to be able to trust them with your thoughts and feelings. You should be able to feel vulnerable around them without worrying about being mocked, rejected, or invalidated. You should also trust them enough to make life-changing decisions with them.

For instance, if you come back from work feeling frustrated, you should be able to share your emotions with your partner. Your partner should listen attentively and offer all the emotional support you need without judging or invalidating your feelings.

Effective Communication

Maintaining a relationship is a breeze during the good times. Recognizing whether you're in a healthy relationship can only be determined by assessing how you navigate the tough times together. In a healthy relationship, both partners should be able to express their feelings and actively listen to each other's points of view. Their main goal when arguing should be to find a solution rather than attack each other. Both partners should feel heard, and the solution should satisfy each of them. This way, neither of them would feel resentful. When a common ground can't be found, they should both feel comfortable agreeing to disagree.

Suppose you disagree about how you manage your household finances, for example. In that case, you and your partner should share your concerns and perspectives openly. Considering these factors, you should work on creating a budget and spending strategy that addresses each of your needs and goals.

Forgiveness

Some people don't learn about forgiveness in childhood, especially if they grew up in a very strict or unhealthy household. Forgiveness, however, is key to building healthy and lasting relationships. If you continuously hold grudges against your partner, you'll never fully move on from your problems and slowly start resenting them.

Mutual Enjoyment and Support

Relationships come with their fair share of challenges. These difficulties can be hard to tolerate and navigate if you don't try to enjoy each other's company. The less fun you have together, the less these problems feel worth fighting for. You don't have to have the same passions as your partner, but you should both at least have a few mutual interests. You should also make an effort to show interest in each other's passions and be supportive of one another's individual goals.

Your relationship should also leave room for personal growth and development. You should find the balance between doing things you both love and giving each other space, as well as supporting one another with things that aren't necessarily a common interest. If you both like going to the gym, you can make it a habit to go with each other every day. If you like painting and your partner doesn't, they should still give you the space to practice your hobby and support your growth in this area.

Activity: Relationship Inventory

Assess your current relationships based on what you have learned about unhealthy and healthy relationships.

Strengths: What are you proud of in your current relationships? In which areas do you feel respected, supported, and understood? Which behaviors do you and others exhibit, or in which instances do you feel that you maintain healthy interactions?

Areas for improvement: In which areas can your relationships improve? Do you struggle with any communication challenges, trust issues, etc.? What steps can you take to address these problems?

Activity: Relationship Vision Board

Create a vision board of your ideal healthy relationship. Use image cut-outs, words, drawings, or symbols. Explore your relationship goals, synthesize from several sources, discuss your thoughts and aspirations with your therapist, and create a vision board that reminds you of these desires. This will remind you of what you deserve in a relationship and set reasonable intentions for your current and future interactions.

A vision board helps motivate you as you visualize your goals.
ATTRIBUTION-NONCOMMERCIAL 2.0 GENERIC CC BY-NC 2.0
<*https://creativecommons.org/licenses/by-nc/2.0/* >
https://www.flickr.com/photos/sharisberries/25118543558

Now that you've read this chapter, you understand what a healthy relationship looks like and know how to seek and build connections in which you can thrive. You're ready to work on developing healthy relational patterns and take pride in becoming a happy, fulfilled, and successful person.

Conclusion

Reading this book and answering the questions within it is a great success on its own. Acknowledging that you're struggling with codependency is a difficult realization. Addressing this issue and delving into your traumas requires great courage. It speaks volumes about your commitment to enhancing your well-being and quality of life. You're ready to transform your life and take actionable steps toward becoming a better version of yourself. Take a few minutes to reflect on this incredible journey. Before flipping through this book's pages, reflect on your thoughts and feelings and explore how they're different from your current ones.

Throughout this book, you've come face-to-face with challenging truths, explored complex emotions, and looked into your negative thoughts and all the reasons behind them. You looked within and faced your insecurities and fears. Not only did this help you understand them better, but it also gave you a better understanding of your strengths and resilience. Looking inward is the first step toward breaking free from the shackles of codependency.

Reading this book also gave you the insights and self-awareness to take control of your future without resorting to unhealthy coping mechanisms like codependency. You understand how to build healthy, lasting relationships with people who respect your needs and boundaries. Reading this book, you should realize that you're worthy of practicing self-love, care, and compassion.

As you continue your journey, the most important thing to remember is that healing and recovery aren't a linear process. There will be days when you feel your best and feel tangible progress and change in your life. However, there will be other days when you experience doubts and setbacks. You might feel the need to go back to your old ways instead of exerting the needed effort to make changes.

When this feeling arises, you need to remind yourself that you don't want to return to the way it was because you were happier or it wasn't that bad but because it was comfortable. This was how you've lived, felt, and thought for as long as you remember, so it only makes sense that you'd feel comfortable living that way, even if it's not what's best for you. Each challenge in your healing journey is an opportunity for growth. Embrace these setbacks, try to bounce back, and honor your resilience and progress. Most importantly, remember that you're not alone.

If you enjoyed this book, I'd greatly appreciate a review on Amazon because it helps me to create more books that people want. It would mean a lot to hear from you.

To leave a review:
1. Open your camera app.
2. Point your mobile device at the QR code.
3. The review page will appear in your web browser.

Thanks for your support!

Here's another book by Andy Gardner that you might like

Free Bonus from Andy Gardner

Hi!

My name is Andy Gardner, and first off, I want to THANK YOU for reading my book.

Now you have a chance to join my exclusive email list related to human psychology and self-development so you can get the ebook below for free as well as the potential to get more ebooks for free! Simply click the link below to join.

P.S. Remember that it's 100% free to join the list.

Access your free bonuses here:
https://livetolearn.lpages.co/andy-gardner-codependency-recovery-workbook-paperback/

Or, Scan the QR code!

References

11 Signs You Are Codependent. (2017, July 24). Montreal Therapy Centre. https://www.montrealtherapy.com/11-signs-codependent/

5 Ways to Heal a Fear of Abandonment. (n.d.). Chris Rackliffe. https://www.crackliffe.com/words/2022/7/14/how-to-heal-fear-of-abandonment

A Guide to Caring for Yourself While Caring for Others. (n.d.). Trying Together. https://tryingtogether.org/dap/a-guide-to-caring-for-yourself-while-caring-for-others/

A11. Leaves on the Stream Exercise. (n.d.). ACT For Psychosis Recovery. https://actforpsychosis.com/pdfs/A11_Leaves_on_the_stream.pdf

AB, P. S. (n.d.). What are the signs of poor communication in a relationship? | Remainly. Www.remainly.com. https://www.remainly.com/articles/what-are-the-signs-of-poor-communication-in-a-relationship

Abandonment issues: Signs, symptoms, treatment, and more. (2022, September 9). Www.medicalnewstoday.com. https://www.medicalnewstoday.com/articles/abandonment-issues#impact

Abumaria, L. M. (2016, November 28). Recognizing Self-Neglect. Self-Neglect. https://selfneglect.org/self-neglect-facts/self-neglect-basics/recognizing-self-neglect/

Adams, A. (2023, June 12). 7 Components of Effective Professional Communication - Virginia Ready. Virginiaready.org. https://virginiaready.org/resources/7-components-of-effective-professional-communication/

Aster, H. (2022, January 11). Seeking Validation From Others Won't Make You Happy. Shortform Books. https://www.shortform.com/blog/seeking-validation-from-others/

Avoiding Assumptions…How to Ask! (2018, July 3). Practice Solutions Blog. https://practicesolutionsinc.net/blog/2018/07/avoiding-assumptions/

Barbara Field. (2023, April 23). Overcoming Feelings of Resentment in Your Relationships. Verywell Mind. https://www.verywellmind.com/how-to-cope-with-resentment-in-relationships-7371451

Beattie, M. (2009). Codependent No More. Phoenix Books Inc.

BetterHelp Editorial Team. (2022, July 14). Learning How To Recognize Codependency And Tips For Preventing It | BetterHelp. Betterhelp.com; BetterHelp. https://www.betterhelp.com/advice/general/learning-how-to-recognize-codependency-and-tips-for-preventing-it/

BetterHelp Editorial Team. (n.d.). How A Fear Of Abandonment Can Affect A Relationship | BetterHelp. Www.betterhelp.com.

https://www.betterhelp.com/advice/phobias/how-a-fear-of-abandonment-can-affect-a-relationship/

Bjelland, J. (2024, February 4). The Silent Neglect: How Ignoring Your Needs Can Lead to Burnout. Julie Bjelland. https://www.juliebjelland.com/hsp-blog/the-silent-neglect-how-ignoring-your-needs-can-lead-to-burnout

Britton, J. (2019, March 18). 5 Steps to Communicate Your Needs to Your Friends (Without Feeling Needy). Yellow Co. https://archive.yellowco.co/blog/2019/03/18/5-steps-communicate-needs-friends-without-feeling-needy/

Celestine, N. (2021, November 13). How to Begin Your Self-Discovery Journey: 16 Best Questions. PositivePsychology.com. https://positivepsychology.com/self-discovery/

Characteristics of Healthy & Unhealthy Relationships | Youth.gov. (n.d.). https://youth.gov/youth-topics/teen-dating-violence/characteristics

Cherry, K. (2023). Types of Nonverbal Communication. Verywell Mind. https://www.verywellmind.com/types-of-nonverbal-communication-2795397

Clinic, C. (2023, December 19). 12 Signs You're in a Healthy Relationship. Cleveland Clinic. https://health.clevelandclinic.org/signs-of-a-healthy-relationship

Co-Dependency. (n.d.). Mental Health America. https://www.mhanational.org/co-dependency

Codependency and the Need to Create Boundaries. (2022, July 15). Next Level Recovery. https://www.nextlevelrecoveryassociates.com/blog-posts/codependency-and-the-need-to-create-boundaries

Codependency. (2023a, June 26). Psychology Today. https://www.psychologytoday.com/us/basics/codependency

Codependency: Signs, Causes, and Help - HelpGuide.org. (n.d.). Https://Www.helpguide.org. https://www.helpguide.org/articles/relationships-communication/codependency.htm

Cox, J. (2016, May 17). Recovery from Codependency. Psych Central. https://psychcentral.com/relationships/recovery-from-codependency

Cox, J. (2022, July 21). Leaning into Recovery from Codependency. Psych Central. https://psychcentral.com/relationships/recovery-from-codependency#codependency-recovery

Cuncic, A. (2022, November 9). What is active listening? Verywell Mind. https://www.verywellmind.com/what-is-active-listening-3024343#toc-7-active-listening-techniques

Das, T. (2024, February 5). Types of unhealthy communication patterns: 4 ways to improve them. Hindustan Times. https://www.hindustantimes.com/lifestyle/relationships/types-of-unhealthy-communication-patterns-4-ways-to-improve-them-101707144146046.html

Deaner, C. (n.d.). Codependency - Who Am I Without Others? Cheryl Deaner. https://www.cheryldeaner.com/codependency-who-am-i-without-others

DeBonis, K. (2021, July 14). Fear of abandonment. What people-pleasers should know. Karen DeBonis. https://karendebonis.com/fear-of-abandonment/

DipLC, K. P. B., MA. (2021, February 24). Abandonment Issues and Low Self-Esteem. More Self-Esteem. https://more-selfesteem.com/more-self-esteem/building-self-esteem/how-does-low-self-esteem-affect-relationships/abandonment-issues-and-low-self-esteem/#google_vignette

Eisler, M. (2018, June 2). Ease Anxiety with These 5 Visualization Techniques. Mindful Minutes. https://mindfulminutes.com/ease-anxiety-with-visualization-techniques/

Faiza Yasir. (2023, September 4). The Power of Effective Communication: Building Stronger Relationships. Medium. https://medium.com/@faizayasir299/the-power-of-effective-communication-building-stronger-relationships-c82a38a397ac

Fritscher, L. (n.d.). Why Some People Experience a Fear of Abandonment. Verywell Mind. https://www.verywellmind.com/fear-of-abandonment-2671741#toc-symptoms-of-fear-of-abandonment

Gillette, H. (2023, August 23). 5 common causes of codependency. Psych Central. https://psychcentral.com/health/what-causes-codependency#demanding-situations

Gould, W. R. (2020, December 8). What Is Codependency? Verywell Mind. https://www.verywellmind.com/what-is-codependency-5072124

Haupt, A. (2023, November 8). Is your family codependent? 8 signs to look out for. TIME. https://time.com/6331335/is-family-codependent/

Hovde, M. (2022, September 28). Self-Exploration: Benefits and Tips for Getting Started. Psych Central. https://psychcentral.com/blog/self-exploration-getting-to-know-thyself

How Past Memories Can Negatively Impact Your Future Relationships | Regain. (2023, September 12). https://www.regain.us/advice/general/how-past-memories-can-negatively-impact-your-future-relationships/

How Trauma Can Result in Codependency. (2020, August 14). https://www.brightquest.com/blog/how-trauma-can-result-in-codependency/

Indita, H. (2022, October 25). Our Past Relationship Can Shape the Way We Love in Our Next One. Inspire. https://www.cxomedia.id/love-and-relationship/20221025151511-92-176753/our-past-relationship-can-shape-the-way-we-love-in-our-next-one

J G A, M. (2023, October 6). From External Approval to Inner Assurance: Breaking the Validation Cycle. Www.linkedin.com.

https://www.linkedin.com/pulse/from-external-approval-inner-assurance-breaking-validation-j-g-a/

Jenner, D. N. (2022, August 29). Conflict Management For The Codependent. FREE from CODEPENDENCY. https://freefromcodependency.com/2022/08/29/conflict-management-for-the-codependent/

Kariuki, D. C. (2023, May 17). The Art of Effective Communication: Enhancing Relationships and Achieving Results. Www.linkedin.com. https://www.linkedin.com/pulse/art-effective-communication-enhancing-relationships-evolution-/

Khot, M. (2023, February 15). How to Practice Kundalini Meditation. Avaana Answers. https://avaana.com.au/blog/kundalini-meditation/

Killoren, C. (2021, December 20). 7 Steps to Building an Interdependent Relationship With Your Partner - Relish. Relish. https://hellorelish.com/articles/interdependent-relationships.html

Kimball, S. (2021, January 7). Do You Have Poor Communication In Your Relationship? Here Are 5 Signs. Sass Magazine. https://sassmagazine.com/do-you-have-poor-communication-in-your-relationship-here-are-5-signs/

Krauss Whitbourne, S. (2023, September 12). Why Constantly Seeking Approval Can Kill a Relationship | Psychology Today. Www.psychologytoday.com. https://www.psychologytoday.com/intl/blog/fulfillment-at-any-age/202308/why-constantly-seeking-approval-is-bad-for-your-relationship

Lancer, D. (2020, December 15). The Cause and Signs of a Lost Self: Emptiness, Depression and Codependency. Becoming You. https://medium.com/becoming-you/the-cause-and-signs-of-a-lost-self-emptiness-depression-and-codependency-4cdc578901b9

Lewandowski, G. W., Jr, & Sahner, D. (2005). The influence of past relationships on subsequent relationships: The role of the self. ResearchGate. https://www.researchgate.net/publication/290264995_The_influence_of_past_relationships_on_subsequent_relationships_The_role_of_the_self

Li, P. (2024, January 23). Childhood Emotional Neglect: 20 Signs, Examples & How To Heal. Parenting for Brain. https://www.parentingforbrain.com/childhood-emotional-neglect/

LMFT, D. L., JD. (2016, April 9). 6 Keys to Assertive Communication. What Is Codependency? https://whatiscodependency.com/6-keys-to-assertive-communication/

LMFT, D. L., JD. (2018, April 30). Do I Have to Lose Me to Love You? What Is Codependency? https://whatiscodependency.com/lost-self-codependent-relationships/

Lockett, E. (2022, October 20). What Is a Codependent Relationship? Could I Be in One? Healthline.
https://www.healthline.com/health/relationships/codependent-relationship

M. Darcy, A. (2016, August 16). Fear of Abandonment - 12 Signs it is Secretly Sabotaging Your Relationships. Harley TherapyTM Blog.
https://www.harleytherapy.co.uk/counselling/fear-of-abandonment.htm

Marshall, T. (2023, September 21). 10 Simple Ways to Grow a Relationship and Thrive as a Couple. Possibility Change. https://possibilitychange.com/10-simple-powerful-ways-to-grow-a-relationship/

Martin, S. (2021, December 17). Healthy Dependency vs. Codependency. Live Well With Sharon Martin. https://www.livewellwithsharonmartin.com/healthy-dependency-vs-codependency/

Matijasevic, M. (2022, January 24). Why Self Discovery Is Hard: Challenges of Owning Your Truth | Markooo. https://markooo.com/why-is-self-discovery-hard/

Mc Guinness, C. (2020, October 5). 10 important elements to effective communication in 2020! Www.linkedin.com.
https://www.linkedin.com/pulse/10-important-elements-effective-communication-2020-mc-guinness/

News-Medical. (2019, June 19). Psychiatrist explains how the brain blocks memory to help get through traumatic event. https://www.news-medical.net/news/20161209/Psychiatrist-explains-how-the-brain-blocks-memory-to-help-get-through-traumatic-ev ent.aspx

Nguyen, J. (2021, October 6). 9 Signs You Might Be The "Clingy" One In Your Relationships. Mindbodygreen.
https://www.mindbodygreen.com/articles/being-clingy-in-relationships

Nunez, K. (2020, November 9). Breath of Fire Yoga: Benefits and How to Do It Correctly. Healthline. https://www.healthline.com/health/breath-of-fire-yoga#how-to-do-it

Odell, C. A. (n.d.). How is Life Tree(ting) You?: Trust, Safety, and Respect - The Importance of Boundaries | Student Affairs. Studentaffairs.stanford.edu. https://studentaffairs.stanford.edu/how-life-treeting-you-importance-of-boundaries#:~:text=Boundaries%20help%20determine%20what%20is

Passfield, R. (n.d.). How to Overcome being Imprisoned by Self-Neglect – Grow Mindfulness. Growmindfulness.com. https://growmindfulness.com/how-to-overcome-being-imprisoned-by-self-neglect/

Phxman. (2023, October 13). Navigating the Depths Within: Exploring Self-Exploration. Phnxman. https://www.phnxman.com/self-exploration/

Pietrangelo, A. (2019, February 13). What Is Fear of Abandonment, and Can It Be Treated? Healthline; Healthline Media.

https://www.healthline.com/health/fear-of-abandonment

Ratson, M., & Garbacz, A. (2023, August 15). Interdependent Relationship: Characteristics, Examples, & More. WikiHow. https://www.wikihow.com/Interdependent-Relationship

Reid, S. (2023, December 19). Codependency - HelpGuide.org. Https://Www.helpguide.org. https://www.helpguide.org/articles/relationships-communication/codependency.htm

relationship.fluent. (2023, May 5). 5 Big Reasons For The Importance Of Communication In Relationships. Relationship Fluent. https://relationshipfluent.com/importance-of-communication-in-relationships/

Rice, M. (2022, September 20). Exploring the Fear of Abandonment. Talkspace. https://www.talkspace.com/blog/fear-of-abandonment/

Rosario, T. M. D. (2022, October 27). The Power Of Communication In A Relationship. Healing Collective. https://www.healingcollectivetherapy.com/resources/power-of-communication-in-relationship

S, A. (2021, December 21). 9 Signs Of Bad Communication In A Relationship. Bonobology.com. https://www.bonobology.com/signs-bad-communication-in-relationship/

Schmidt, K. (2022, March 4). Handling Confrontation Anxiety: How to overcome the fear of conflict. Www.linkedin.com. https://www.linkedin.com/pulse/handling-confrontation-anxiety-how-overcome-fear-conflict-schmidt/

Scott, E. (n.d.). 5 Simple Steps to Assertive Communication. Verywell Mind. https://www.verywellmind.com/learn-assertive-communication-in-five-simple-steps-3144969#toc-how-to-develop-an-assertive-communication-style

Self-Care Checklist Counseling and Psychological Services. (n.d.). https://caps.sonoma.edu/sites/caps/files/selfcarecovid-19checklistssucaps2020.pdf

Sinclair, Y. (2011, July 5). Balancing Codependent Tendencies: Improving Relationships through Self-Care. GoodTherapy.org Therapy Blog. https://www.goodtherapy.org/blog/self-care-enhance-relationship/

Smith, K. (2022, May 20). Signs of a Codependent vs. Interdependent Relationship. Psych Central. https://psychcentral.com/lib/codependency-vs-interdependency#can-it-be-changed

Smith, M., MA. (2023, December 19). Codependency: Signs, causes, and help. HelpGuide.org. https://www.helpguide.org/articles/relationships-communication/codependency.htm

Smith, S. (2021, November 9). 15 Signs of a Clingy Partner & How to Stop Being Clingy. Marriage Advice - Expert Marriage Tips & Advice.

https://www.marriage.com/advice/relationship/signs-your-partner-is-too-clingy/

Sophie. (2023, February 19). Seeking Validation | How to Stop Caring What Other People Think. International View. https://intentionalview.com/why-youve-got-to-stop-seeking-external-validation/

Staff, N. I. (2023, July 17). Fear of Abandonment in Young Adults: What It Means and How to Heal. Newport Institute. https://www.newportinstitute.com/resources/mental-health/fear-of-abandonment/

Tanasugarn, A. (2022, October 6). Creating Healthy Interdependence in Your Relationship | Psychology Today. Www.psychologytoday.com. https://www.psychologytoday.com/intl/blog/understanding-ptsd/202210/creating-healthy-interdependence-in-your-relationship

Tanasugarn, A. (n.d.). 5 Unexpected Ways Abandonment Fears Affect Relationships | Psychology Today. Www.psychologytoday.com. https://www.psychologytoday.com/us/blog/understanding-ptsd/202401/5-unexpected-ways-abandonment-fears-affect-relationships

Teplin, J. (2022, November 25). The pros and cons of external validation. Manhattan Wellness. https://manhattanwellness.org/the-pros-and-cons-of-external-validation/

Therapy, E. Y. (2023, February 20). 5 Reasons You Are Developing Codependent Relationships. Embracing You Therapy. https://embracingyoutherapy.com/5-reasons-why-you-may-be-developing-codependent-relationships/

Thien. (2022, December 18). What is a codependent relationship and are you in one? Relationships Australia NSW. https://www.relationshipsnsw.org.au/blog/signs-codependent-relationship/

Webb, J. (2023, July 11). Self-Neglect: A Telltale Sign of Childhood Emotional Neglect | Psychology Today South Africa. Www.psychologytoday.com. https://www.psychologytoday.com/za/blog/childhood-emotional-neglect/202305/self-neglect-a-telltale-sign-of-childhood-emotional-neglect

Wenner-Foy, C. (2022, September 21). Codependency Relationship: A Lack of Genuine Communication! Colleen Wenner. https://florida-counseling.com/codependency-relationship-a-lack-of-genuine-communication/

What Is an Interdependent Relationship? (n.d.). Paired. https://www.paired.com/articles/interdependent-relationship

Whitfield, C. (2010). A Gift to Myself. Simon and Schuster.

Zimberoff, D. (2017). Breaking free from the victim trap: reclaiming your personal power. Wellness Press